FAUSTUS SOCINUS

Faustus Socinus

by
DAVID MUNROE CORY, TH.D.

WIPF & STOCK · Eugene, Oregon

Wipf and Stock Publishers
199 W 8th Ave, Suite 3
Eugene, OR 97401

Faustus Socinus
By Cory, David Munroe
ISBN 13: 978-1-60608-393-2
Publication date 01/05/2009
Previously published by The Beacon Press, 1932

PREFACE

Even such a slender volume as this treatise on the life and work of Faustus Socinus, must, of necessity, be based upon a considerable body of source material and the contributions and comments in later works. In the quest for the literature on the subject, the author has been guided by the wise counsel and wide knowledge of Principal Earl Morse Wilbur, of the Pacific Unitarian School of Theology, and Prof. William Walker Rockwell, Librarian of Union Theological Seminary, New York. Prof. F. J. Foakes Jackson, of Union Seminary, has been of the greatest assistance in the preparation of the manuscript, as advisor on both the literary and historical aspects of the work. The helpful interest of the Rev. John Howland Lathrop, of the Unitarian Church of the Savior, Brooklyn, has also greatly encouraged the author in his undertaking. All these gentlemen have been so good as to read the manuscript in its entirety, and to them the author would attribute such value as this work may have, in presenting to the public the life and labors of a little remembered, but important pioneer in the quest of religious liberty.

BROOKLYN, NEW YORK,

CONTENTS

	PAGE
PREFACE	iii
INTRODUCTION	vii

PART I—THE LIFE OF FAUSTUS SOCINUS.

CHAPTER

    I. The Renaissance and Reformation in North Italy. 1
   II. The Heritage of Socinus. 11
  III. Uncle and Nephew. 19
  IV. The Fallow Years. 27
   V. Controversy in Switzerland and Transylvania. 35
  VI. Poland and the Reformation. 43
 VII. The Rise of Antitrinitarianism in Poland. . . 51
VIII. Socinus in Poland. 59
  IX. Conflict and Consummation. 68
   X. A Gentleman and a Scholar. 76

PART II—THE TEACHING OF FAUSTUS SOCINUS.

   XI. The Norm of Doctrine 85
  XII. God, One in Essence and Lord of All . . . 92
 XIII. Jesus Christ, the Son of God 98
 XIV. Free Obedience, the Way of Life. 106
  XV. Immortality, the Goal of Life. 115
 XVI. True Doctrine, the Test of the True Church. 121
XVII. Socinus and Religious Tolerance. 129
XVIII. Socinus and Pacifism 136
 XIX. The Continuing Influence of Socinus . . . 143

      Bibliography 153

INTRODUCTION

BY

THE REV. PROFESSOR F. J. FOAKES JACKSON, D. D.

There are few religious leaders whose careers are more interesting, or whose personalities are more attractive than the two Sozzini, yet perhaps in hardly any aspect is the Christian religion less inviting than in what is known as Socinianism. For to most the study of any religion, and this is true not only of that of Jesus, but of all faiths, is of interest when it is a force which quickens the imagination of humanity, and brings man in touch with the unseen world, when it inspires them with new ideals of life, when it holds out hopes which cannot here be realized, when it proves a living power to lift the soul into a higher sphere. A religion based solely on reason cannot be expected to influence the heart, or make its votaries capable of heroic even if perverse self sacrifice. It may begin with a fiery repudiation of error, and produce real prophets of scientific thought or poets like Lucretius and Shelley, but it tends inevitably in the end to a frigid indifference to all spiritual interests in their widest sense. If therefore we place the religion of Laelius and Faustus

INTRODUCTION

Socinus in this category, it is small wonder that it fails to have any attraction.

No one who reads Mr. Cory's book can fail to be impressed by his sketch of the Sozzini. Born in Siena, of a noble and intellectual family of scholars and lawyers, Laelius and his nephew, Faustus, left their home owing to their antagonism to the dominant and intolerant Catholicism of Italy, Laelius to make devoted friends wherever he went, and Faustus to find them among the nobility of remote Poland. Faustus, who is the main figure, cannot be understood apart from the age in which he lived, nor may he be ranked among modern skeptics. He and his uncle were the products of the Italian renaissance of the sixteenth century. To Faustus Trinitarianism was repellent, not because it was irrational, but because it was unscriptural. He read his Bible and could not discover in it the theology recognized alike by the Catholics and Protestants of his day. To him Christ appeared too human to be ranked with the Father, and yet too divine for His commands not to be obeyed literally. Thus Faustus Socinus rejected the current theology together with the compromises which strove to reconcile the moral demands of Jesus with the requirements of human society. In this spirit he denounced all war for whatever reason it was engaged in, and all violent methods employed to

INTRODUCTION

secure the well being of the state. This makes the study of his life of especial interest to us of today.

Mr. Cory has endeavoured not only to trace the career of the Sozzini by picturing their lives in northern Italy, Switzerland, and Eastern Europe, and to give the views of Faustus often in his own words, but also to correlate his material with modern thought and aims. He has, in some respects, blazed a new trail which may lead to further developments for himself or others to pursue. The Unitarianism of the Sozzini found a home among the intellectual aristocracy of Poland, and, in a different form, in cultured circles elsewhere, notably in New England, but it never flourished widely among the people. Nevertheless it has had an abiding influence upon the history of progress, humanity and social justice.

Just as the expiatory monument erected a generation ago at Geneva to the memory of Servetus was subscribed to by the Consistory of the Church of Calvin, so it is appropriate that this, the first biography of Socinus to be published in English since 1777, should be the work of a minister of the Presbyterian Church in the United States of America.

PART ONE

THE LIFE OF FAUSTUS SOCINUS

CHAPTER I

THE RENAISSANCE AND REFORMATION IN NORTH ITALY

MODERN historical criticism has dispelled the myth that the capture of Constantinople by the Turks, in 1453, drove into Italy a group of Greek scholars who initiated that great cultural movement known as the Renaissance. Much Greek literature, in the original or translation, had been available for more than two hundred years, and it had not been neglected. Thomas Aquinas, and other great scholars of the thirteenth century, had combined Aristotle with the traditional teaching of the church. Dante, through Virgil, had drunk deep of the classic heritage. A little later, we find the classical interest more strongly marked. Boccaccio studied Greek and secured the appointment of his teacher, Leone Pilato, to the first chair of Greek in an Italian University (Florence). Petrarch, usually styled the "Father of the Renaissance," encouraged the study of the classics and was a devoted student of Cicero. On the other hand, it is true that none of these writers really appreciated, or appropriated, the genius of the classical age. Aquinas' interests were theological, rather than philosophical, and he used Aristotle for purposes alien to the mind of "the Philosopher." Dante, likewise, used Virgil for his own ends, and is the very incarnation of the spirit of the Middle Ages. In the following century, Boccaccio, while deserting the medieval Latin for the *dolce volgare,* was hardly a classical scholar, and is nearer to the French *raconteurs* than to the ancient models of Greek or Latin prose. Petrarch, who confessed that Greek was an enigma to him, went back for his theology to Augustine, rather than to the modernism of Aquinas.

These forerunners of the Renaissance were humanists in the sense that they broke the constraint of a theological or linguistic tradition and reinterpreted life according to new forms, but in relation to the classics of the ancient world, especially the Greek, they were like children playing with new-found toys too advanced for their years. Aquinas is not a disciple of Aristotle, and the founders of Italian literature are not Greek or even Roman in feeling or language, but medieval Italians. It was the rediscovery not merely of the literature, but of the art, and above all of the spirit of the Classic Age in the fifteenth and sixteenth centuries which inaugurated the Renaissance in Italy.

North Italy, studded with its busy and wealthy

RENAISSANCE IN NORTH ITALY

city-states, was a fertile field for the new culture. Her sons adorned their native towns with the treasures of art that still attract crowds of tourists, or flocking to Rome under the patronage of such humanist popes as Nicholas V, Julius II, and Leo X, lavished their talents upon the eternal city.

One of the characteristics of this Renaissance was the remarkable versatility of some of its greatest geniuses. Leon Battista Alberti was a musician, jurist, architect, draftsman, and litterateur. Leonardo da Vinci was an architect, engineer, mathematician, poet, and painter. Michael Angelo was an architect, sculptor, painter, and poet. These men were no mere *dilletanti*, however; they excelled in all these varied fields of endeavor.

It was Florence under the rule of the splendid and pleasure-loving Medici family that fostered the classical studies with the greatest zeal, but it was also Florence with her pure Tuscan speech that preserved and cherished the infant Italian literature. These two streams flowing in parallel courses, like the Tigris and Euphrates in ancient Babylonia, were connected by many canals, and their waters mingled and enriched the land through which they flowed.

A period of aesthetic development is, however, often a period of ethical degeneration. At Florence, Savonarola had declaimed against the train of voluptuous habits that had accompanied the revival of Hellenistic culture, and the Reformation, which shook all Europe in the sixteenth century, was not so much a protest against the Medievalism of the Church as against the abuses that had accompanied its growing secularization in the Renaissance. The loss of most of Northern Europe had for the Catholic Church a sobering effect upon her religious life, and the easy-going humanism of Leo X gave way to the reforming zeal of a series of pious and active pontiffs. The Counter-Reformation wove a new sense of responsibility and coherence into the torn and frayed fabric of the Church, and her loyal servants, the new order of the Jesuits, made every effort to repair the breaches in the lands still predominantly Catholic, and to win back the now powerful and organized Protestants.

Northern Italy had passed through the stage of buoyant humanism in the latter half of the fifteenth and the early part of the sixteenth centuries and was now more soberly adjusting her newfound knowledge and art to the changing political and religious conditions. Emperor and Roman pontiff, after the Treaty of Barcelona in 1529, worked hand in hand, the one dominating Italy politically with viceroys at Milan and Naples, and the other, backed by the civil power of Spain,

RENAISSANCE IN NORTH ITALY

crushing out Protestantism by means of the Inquisition and the activity of the Jesuit order. Only Venice and Genoa, and a couple of insignificant republics, remained free from the Spanish-Papal domination.

Religious questions again assumed the center of the stage, as art, politics, and letters receded into the background.

The Reformation in Italy, unlike that in the North of Europe, owed its origin not so much to the fiery monk who combined his medieval piety with the new spirit of nationalism, or to the painstaking lawyer who envisaged a new moral and social order under the Supreme Sovereign, as to the man of letters—the product of humanism. Speaking of the movement in Italy, Allen declares: "The starting point is not, as before, in the protest of the German Reformers, and not in the bosom of a secluded, obscure, and fanatical sect. It is in the very heart of the Catholic Church itself, in the interior circles of its purest piety and its most refined intelligence."[1]

In the fourteenth and fifteenth centuries, a remarkable freedom of inquiry had prevailed in Europe. So long as the free-thinkers refrained from attacking the Church as an institution, great liberty of theological opinion seems to have been permitted. Nowhere was the spirit of inquiry pushed further than in the cultured circles of

FAUSTUS SOCINUS

North Italy. In the university towns of Florence, Bologna, and especially Padua, a spirit of free investigation and earnest scholarship flourished side by side. The Averroism of Padua had been frowned upon by the Church at large for generations, but that university, secure in Venetian territory, continued in somewhat erratic, but nevertheless honest fashion to explore and expound the wealth of classical and Mohammedan literature. Florence in the fifteenth century had witnessed a sincere though sentimental revival of Neo-Platonism, and her Medici overlords fostered the new "Academy" with their active encouragement and great wealth.

The German Reformation gave the signal for a widespread protest against the corruptions of the Roman Church and the subtleties of scholastic dogma. Reforming preachers like Savonarola had already sowed the seed for a genuine religious awakening, scholars like Pico of Mirandola had revived a burning zeal for the study of the Scriptures. Antonio Bruccioli produced an excellent Italian version of the whole Bible at Venice in 1532, and its popularity was so great that the Roman Church was compelled to answer it with a number of "authorized" versions.

The common note of the various Italian reformers, whether "practical mystics" like Valdes in the beginning of the movement, or "intellectuals" like the Socini at its close, is the freshness of approach. When all is said and done there is very little difference between the theology of Luther and that of the traditional Augustinian position. To be sure, such a scholar as Thomas Aquinas in the thirteenth century had propounded a system more Aristotelian than the Neo-Platonic-Christian synthesis of Augustine, and, in the following century, William of Occam had advocated a kind of empirical nominalism, but the dominant theology of the period was that of Duns Scotus, who had effected a compromise between moderate Aristotelianism and the traditional view. Luther was, theologically speaking, no innovator, but rather a reactionary who, despising the attempts to reconcile faith with the natural order, went back to the period before the thirteenth century. In fact, the great majority of the reformers did not revolt against the beliefs of the Church, but against its authority and corruption. Melanchthon in a celebrated letter to Cardinal Campeggio (July 6, 1530), was anxious to make this plain: "We have no difference with Rome on a single point of dogma."[2]

The Italian reformers, on the other hand, in their emphasis upon personal piety, commenced with ignoring the traditional theology and ended by substituting a new theology in place of the traditional views. Lecky neatly summarizes the movement in its final phases: "The Reformation in Italy was almost confined to a small group of scholars, who preached its principles to their extreme limits, with an unflinching logic, with a disregard for both tradition and consequences, and above all with a secular spirit that was elsewhere unequaled." [3]

The whole movement was characterized by an earnest spirit that appealed to conscience, reason, and Scripture, and deprecated the appeal to external authority to which Luther and Calvin so frequently had recourse.

The pietistic movement, the first stage of the Italian Reformation, was initiated by a cultured Spanish courtier, Juan Valdes; it was distinctly a movement within the Church, and so far as its popular influence was concerned, was confined to Naples. Valdes died before the gathering storm of papal disfavor broke upon him, but his followers, though protected for some time in Naples by local sentiment, were to suffer the terrors of the Inquisition. Bernardino Ochino, one of the most eloquent preachers of North Italy, combined the devotion of his friend Valdes with a spirit of free inquiry and was compelled to flee the country. He traveled an exile from land to land, professing a kind of Unitarianism prophetic of the Universalism of the early nineteenth century. The Reformers, as well as the Catholics, found him sub-

RENAISSANCE IN NORTH ITALY

versive and persecuted him with scarcely less zeal. Worn out, he died at Slavkov (Austerlitz) in Moravia (1565), in his seventy-eighth year.

In the year of Valdes' death (1542), the Inquisition was established in Italy, and a vigorous persecution of the Protestants began. The general claim of leniency for the Inquisition in Italy seems scarcely to be borne out by the facts. In 1567, Pietro Carnesecchi, a Florentine of high character and wide learning, was executed at Rome, and three years later the aged Aonio Paleario of Tuscany met the same fate. Paleario's sphere of greatest influence was in Siena where he delivered popular lectures for a number of years and publicly defended himself against the charges of heresy brought forward by his opponents; no doubt his opinions exercised an important influence on the Socini. His theology was Christocentric as was his character, and his influence continued in the city long after he was forced to quit it (C.1543).[4]

The same alliance of Papal and Spanish interests that led to the suppression of the free life of most of the Italian city-states resulted in the almost complete obliteration of Protestantism in Italy. Exiled congregations and individual reformers, butchered communities and lonely martyrs attest the courage and conviction of the Italian Protestants, but their great work was not to be in their own land, and the greatest among them was to bear witness to the ancient proverb quoted by his Lord that a prophet is not without honor save in his own country.

NOTES

1. Allen—*A History of the Unitarians*, New York, 1894, 5.
2. "Dogma nullum habemus diversum ab ecclesia romana."—*Opera* (C. G. Bretschneider), *Corpus Reformatorum*, Halle, 1835, II, 170.
3. *Rationalism in Europe*, New York, 1914, II, 60.
4. See M. Young, *The Life and Times of Aonio Paleario*, London, 1860, I, 514.

CHAPTER II

THE HERITAGE OF SOCINUS

FAMILY and city—these are the two great foci around which a man's life revolved in the golden age of the city-states of North Italy; in the four hundred years stretching from the middle of the twelfth to the middle of the sixteenth century we see a colorful picture of the rise and fall of brilliant cities and their brilliant families.

The achievements of the ancestors of Socinus are woven together in a striking pattern in the history of Siena. In this beautiful city they lived and loved, legislated and lorded, and finally lost all. The lad Faustus grew up amid mighty memories—memories that were essentially secular, for even the churchmen in his family were greater as statesmen and scholars than as saints. Scholarship, but not scholasticism, piety rather than sanctity, great memories rather than glowing prospects, composed the atmosphere of the boyhood of the reformer. His sweet mother, Agnese Petrucci, brought him up at the quiet country seat of the family at Scopeto, and his paternal grandfather and uncles took a keen interest in the promising youth. No doubt the lad reflected upon the past glories of his city and family, and resolved that he would make his mark in the world. The political field was barred by the iron hand of Spanish tyranny, the church was closed to a free spirit like Socinus by its tightening orthodoxy and growing distrust of the "false Renaissance," the law held out no attractions for such an active temperament, art had entered upon a decadent period, and only letters, unless we may add speculation, offered inviting avenues for the young adventurer.

Throughout the latter portion of the Middle Ages, Tuscany was a geographical rather than a political unit. The struggle between the emperors and the Popes enabled the growing cities to assert their own independence and to develop their governments along republican lines. Chief among the five Tuscan cities was Florence; of scarcely less importance were Pisa and Siena.

In the twelfth century, after a long period of ducal and ecclesiastical domination, Siena became a republic, and for five generations was the scene of civil conflict between the nobles who sided with the emperors and the burghers who supported the Popes. During this stormy period the cathedral was begun and in 1203 the university was founded. The fact that the faculties of the university were limited to law and medicine, had a

THE HERITAGE OF SOCINUS

lasting influence upon the tastes and temper of the people. It was not until 1321, however, that Siena took her place beside the other university towns of Italy. In that year there was an influx of scholars from Bologna who greatly strengthened the faculty of laws. Significantly enough, the Socini, originally a commercial family, arrived in Siena about the same time, and in the following century began that great succession of legal scholars with Mariano Sozzini (the Elder).

From 1285 on, the burghers were supreme over the nobility, but quarrels soon began between the wealthier burghers and the poorer citizens, and after a century of conflict a compromise government resulted.

The fourteenth century gave Siena one of her most famous children, St. Catherine. In the brief space of thirty-three years, this strong-willed saint seems to have succeeded in experiencing far greater austerities under Dominican tutelage than St. Francis ever achieved, or wanted to achieve, and even modern historians do not wholly deny the legend that her visit to Avignon was responsible for the restoration of the Papacy to Rome. This saint left extensive writings which are more notable on literary grounds than for any great depth of devotional or intellectual insight, and the influence of her life and writings upon the Socini seems to have been absolutely "nil."

FAUSTUS SOCINUS

The fifteenth century was another turbulent epoch in the history of Siena, and the dominant ecclesiastical, legal, and political interests kept the city far behind Florence in artistic and literary productions. In the spheres of the Church, the law, and the state, the Sienese certainly held their own, and it is most significant that the three outstanding families in each of these three respects, are found among the immediate forbears of Faustus Socinus.

A typical figure of the century, humanist and churchman, was the ecclesiastical knight-errant, Aeneas Sylvius Piccolomini. After a brilliant though somewhat questionable career, this able Sienese noble was elevated to the Papacy as Pius II. The brilliant scholar and adventurer showed that he could also be a pious and able pope, but he maintained his literary and picturesque character to the end, and died while on the eve of a Crusade against the victorious Turks who had just captured Constantinople. The maternal grandmother of Faustus Socinus, an able and virtuous lady who seems to have exerted a pronounced influence upon him in his childhood, was a niece of this pope, and first cousin of the obscure Pius III.

The mother of Faustus Socinus, Agnese Petrucci, came of that great burgher family that dominated Sienese politics during the last decade of the fifteenth and the first quarter of the six-

THE HERITAGE OF SOCINUS

teenth centuries; Pandolfo Petrucci, her grandfather, was the unscrupulous, but able political boss of the city for more than twenty years, until his death in 1512. His son, Borghese, the father of Agnese, proved oppressive and unpopular and was exiled from the city. A hostile cousin, the Cardinal Raffaello Petrucci, succeeded to power with papal backing, and oppressed the family of Pandolfo. Borghese's younger brother, Fabio, returned to the headship after the death of the cardinal in 1522. The Sienese, who could tolerate the coöperation of genuine *gentiluomini* like the Piccolomini, were disgusted by the pretensions of *Noveschi* burghers like the Petrucci and drove that family from power in December, 1524.

Compared with the Piccolomini, or even the Petrucci, the Socini (Ital. *Sozzini*)[1] could boast no ancient lineage. The earliest known member of the family lived in the little town of Percena where he was engaged in money-lending, an occupation scarcely reputable in the thirteenth century. His second son, Mino Sozzo, settled in Siena,[2] and a century later his descendants had earned a deservedly high reputation. Mariano Sozzini, the Elder (1401-1467), was the greatest jurist of his day. Having married the lovely Niccola Venturi when still a law student, the young man "cut" his classes rather frequently and was called on the carpet by his professor to explain.

FAUSTUS SOCINUS

"I have married a wife," was Mariano's simple excuse. "Well," said the professor, "Socrates was married, too." "Ah," replied the budding lawyer, "Xanthippe was a scold, and I dare say ugly at that; while my wife is both beautiful and sweet-tempered." After graduation, Mariano taught canon law at Padua and later at Siena, and served his native city in many honorable capacities. His solid learning, coupled with a ready wit, made him a favorite everywhere, and he was held in the highest regard by Pius II. Bayle terms this Mariano "the most universal man of his century." [3]

Mariano's son, Bartolommeo, continued the legal reputation of the family; he held chairs successively in Siena, Pisa, Ferrara, Bologna, and finally Pisa again. A true son of the Renaissance, Bartolommeo, though termed "the Papinian of his age," succumbed to its vices, which ruined his scholarship and hastened his death (1507).

Bartolommeo's son, Mariano the younger, the grandfather of Faustus Socinus whom he brought up, had a long and eventful life (1482-1556). He married the young and beautiful Camilla Salvetti, daughter of a powerful Florentine house allied to the Petrucci; she bore him thirteen children, and their forty-six years of happy married life were marred only by political and later by religious persecution. Mariano's legal career was varied and brilliant. At the age of twenty-one he received his

THE HERITAGE OF SOCINUS

doctorate in jurisprudence from Siena and taught there for many years; he was later called to Pisa where he lectured for seven years, only to be recalled to Siena. Mariano soon quitted his native city, owing probably to its disturbed political condition, and in his closing years he held professorships successively at Padua and Bologna, where he died in 1556. The father of Faustus Socinus, Alessandro, was the favorite son of this Mariano. Though dying at the early age of thirty, Alessandro had made a great reputation in the law, the father and son being known as *principes subtilitatum Juris Consultorum*.[4]

The fortunes of all three families were clouded by the political downfall of Siena in 1555, when the city capitulated to the Imperial forces.[5] Thenceforth Siena was an integral part of the Grand Duchy of Tuscany, and Florence became the sole center of political life in the duchy. The power of the Piccolomini gradually waned at the Papal Court, the Petrucci were virtually exiles, the Sozzini saw their political hopes blasted, and the family of Mariano soon fell under the ban of the Inquisition. In such an atmosphere of great memories and gloomy prospects was born and reared Faustus Socinus.

NOTES

1. In view of the general usage of the Latin form *Socinus*, it has been considered wise to employ it rather than the Italian form, when

FAUSTUS SOCINUS

referring to the two reformers. For the same reason, the forms *Laelius* and *Faustus,* rather than Lelio or Fausto are used. Generally speaking, the original Italian, Polish, etc. forms have been retained, exceptions being made when general usage required.

2. The town house of the family, the Palazzo Sozzini, still stands at the corner of the Via Ricasoli and the Via di Follonica, although it is now incorporated with the adjoining Palazzo Malavolti.

3. *Dictionnaire,* Amsterdam, 1734, Vol. V, p. 164. Bayle relates the humorous little incident of Mariano's university days and gives two earlier sources.

4. Toulmin's encomium appears to be fully merited (*Memoirs of Faustus Socinus,* London, 1777, 1).

"His [Faustus'] father was Alexander Socinus, in whom were joined, to an extraordinary force of genius, a most retentive memory and persuasive eloquence. This Alexander Socinus was honored with a diploma by the University of Siena in the year 1530, conferring on him the degree of Doctor of the Civil and Canon Law; was soon after made Professor in ordinary in the University of Padua, and died in the thirty-first year of his age, regretted by all Italy."

Alessandro had two children besides Faustus, who seems to have been the eldest—a son, Alessandro, who became a lawyer and who remained a good Catholic all his life, receiving the highest civic rank that Siena could bestow in 1603, and a daughter, Fillide, who married into the Marsili family.

5. This final bid for freedom and the heroic defence of the citizens following the defeat of their forces at Marciano, is chronicled by one of the Sozzini, Alessandro di Girolamo, in his vivid and sympathetic account: *Il Diario dell' ultima Guerra Senese.* See article *Siena, Ency. Brit.,* IX Ed.

CHAPTER III

UNCLE AND NEPHEW

MARIANO Junior and his lovely wife Camilla were blessed with thirteen children most of whom were sons who ably sustained the cultural reputation of the family. Laelius (Lelio), the sixth son, born in 1525, was destined for a legal career, but the young man, with that inquiring spirit that marked his whole life, abandoned the formal study of jurisprudence for a painstaking examination of the Bible. Laelius Socinus felt that the source of all law, civil and moral, was to be found in Scripture, and not satisfied with the Vulgate or the excellent Italian translations recently produced, he studied Greek, Hebrew, and even Arabic, in order more perfectly to arrive at the exact meaning of the texts. The strong Protestant movement in North Italy attracted the young student, and he became one of its most active supporters.

The evangelical awakening in North Italy, which centered around the brilliant preachers, Ochino and Paleario, both of whom were Tuscans, is the high-water mark of the Italian Reformation. Many converts were won in Venice,

FAUSTUS SOCINUS

Vicenza, Padua, and Siena, and there appears to have been a considerable following *sub rosa* within the Church itself; but the establishment of the Inquisition at Rome in 1542, at the instigation of the zealous Caraffa, nipped the movement in the bud. Cardinal Contarini, who openly favored the reformers, died mysteriously, some said, of poison. Ochino was summoned to Rome, but fled the country; Vermigli (Peter Martyr) and Curione also escaped; Paleario retired to Lucca to the comparative obscurity of a professor's chair, but when he ventured into the more dangerous territory of Milan he was betrayed by the unscrupulous Duke into the hands of the inquisitors and was executed in his old age at Rome.

While the Socini were not as yet under the ban of the Inquisition, Laelius must have felt the storm approaching and left Italy in search of a more congenial atmosphere in which he might pursue his studies and air his views. From 1547 to 1552, the Sienese reformer was absent from Italy, and these years were spent in intensive study and extensive travel in Switzerland, France, England, Holland, Germany, Bohemia, Austria, and even Poland in 1551. Everywhere Laelius' family connections, his culture, his attractiveness, and his earnest spirit won him friends. Every one of the prominent reformers save Zwingli, who had long been dead, and Luther, who had just

UNCLE AND NEPHEW

passed away, was numbered among the friends and correspondents of this amiable Italian; Melanchthon and Bullinger appear to have been his most intimate associates, and even the great head of the Genevan church entertained a high regard for the young man. Much has been written upon the relation of Calvin to Laelius Socinus, and opinion has wavered between two extreme positions, neither of which appears to be correct. Calvin undoubtedly liked the young man and respected his learning and zeal, but rather feared the extent to which he pushed his inquiries. The heresy of Servetus was rife during all this period, and Calvin may have detected resemblances between the Spanish and the Italian radicals; accordingly he sent warning letters, friendly enough in tone, to Laelius, and urged Bullinger to keep an eye on him. Calvin's subsequent suspicions, provoked by some rash statements on the part of Laelius, were with difficulty allayed, but a letter to Bullinger in which Calvin declared that 'he willingly readmitted the now tranquilized Socinus to his friendship, seeing that he had renounced his errors,'[1] shows the good feeling on the part of the great reformer. The reconciliation is further attested by a letter in which Laelius is commended to the patron of the Reformed Church in Poland, Prince Radziwill.

Almost the only active opposition offered to

FAUSTUS SOCINUS

Laelius Socinus on this "triumphal tour" came from his fellow Italian reformers, Martinengo and Vergerio; whether this was due to personal jealousy or to a more adequate knowledge of the real views of Laelius, is an open question.

Siena's brief bid for freedom in 1552 drew Laelius back to his native city, where he found his young nephew Faustus "a lad of parts." Born December 5, 1539, the boy was only about thirteen years younger than his uncle, and a strong bond of friendship was forged between them. Faustus had been carefully brought up at the country seat of the family at Scopeto under the tutelage of his mother and paternal grandmother.[2] Owing perhaps to the troubled political situation his formal education had been somewhat neglected. Years later when writing to a friend, Faustus modestly referred to himself as "a man who never studied philosophy, and who never came in contact with what is called scholastic theology, and who touched nothing of the art of logic save certain rudiments, and crudely at that."[3] There had been little of the Catholic tradition in the nurture of the young Socinus; evangelical opinions had been embraced by nearly all his family, even by such a prominent member as his uncle Celso, who outwardly conformed to the church. In a letter to his Polish benefactor, Martin Wadowitz, Socinus, denying that he had ever deserted the Roman

UNCLE AND NEPHEW

Church, declared "It can scarcely be said that I ever adhered to the Roman Church, since as soon as I came of an age to exercise judgment in religious matters, I was brought up and instructed otherwise than as the Roman Church teaches."[4]

Laelius' visit appears to have made a lasting impression upon his nephew. Faustus was at that age when hero-worship is natural and life decisions are made, and the Catholic writer,[5] who declared that when only thirteen he abandoned his ordinary studies for theology, owing to the influence of his uncle, while ignoring Faustus' continuing interest in literature, is hardly overstating the case. Laelius' departure to Padua and Bologna (where he visited his aged father) and his subsequent return to Zürich did not quench the friendship kindled, and an extensive correspondence only fanned the flame.

Laelius' subsequent career resembled his first tour. Always eager and inquisitive, he pushed his investigations and travels in all directions. His most important trip was another visit paid to Poland in 1558; commended by Calvin to the Polish Protestants, he found a ready welcome and conferred with many of the left-wing leaders there.

Siena's political downfall did not affect her cultural position, and with the encouragement of his uncle, Celso, Faustus became identified with

FAUSTUS SOCINUS

various literary groups, notably the *Accademia degli intronati*. The academic name, *Il Frastagliato*, the badge *Un mare turbato da venti*, and the motto: *Turbant sed extollunt*, assumed by the young man upon his initiation, suggest a volatile, but idealistic temperament, a view that is supported by contemporary evidence.[6]

The heavy hand of the Inquisition was soon felt in these liberal circles in Siena which were proving such a natural breeding ground for unorthodox opinions. Celso Sozzini conformed, Camillo fled, and Cornelio was imprisoned in Rome. Faustus, scarcely more than a youth, appears to have conformed and to have remained unmolested, but he wisely left the city in 1561 for Lyons. He had inherited a fourth part of the estate left by his grandfather, who had died five years before, and probably was engaged in business. There is no special reason to assume that the young man had gone to Lyons to be near Laelius, although a visit or two was exchanged between them. If this had been the governing motive in Faustus' departure from Siena, he could have as easily gone to Switzerland.

Laelius, who had returned to Zürich, died unexpectedly in May, 1562, to the great sorrow of his nephew, who hastened to that city to pay his respects to the memory of his uncle and to dispose of his personal property. Laelius had not inher-

UNCLE AND NEPHEW

ited any of the patrimony of Mariano, and Faustus' visit must have been impelled by a feeling of love and duty, and also a desire to procure his uncle's literary remains. These were neither extensive nor important, and the fiction, that in them Faustus suddenly came upon a full-blown heresy, is without foundation. The younger man was always ready to concede, and even to overestimate his debt to Laelius, and their frequent correspondence no doubt contributed to the theological bent of the nephew, but the paucity of Laelius' literary achievements, to say nothing of the fragmentary and tentative character of his opinions, renders the oft-asserted charge of plagiarism on the part of Faustus improbable.[7]

NOTES

1. *The Life and Times of John Calvin,* by Paul Henry, D.D., London, 1849, II, 350.
2. *Opera,* I, 490^a.
3. *Opera,* I, 476^b.
4. Guichard, *Histoire du Socinianisme,* Paris, 1723.
5. Much of the interesting but rather gossipy history of the Socini is derived from a long work by a certain Panzirol, published in Latin, but with extensive quotations in Italian, *De Claris Legum Interpp.* (1637). Bayle and Gordon have discovered various references to the ancestors and early days of Faustus Socinus in this rambling work.
6. Gordon (Article, Socinus II, *Encyclopaedia Brittanica,* summarises Faustus' debt to his uncle as follows: "(1) He derived from him in conversation (1552-53) the germ of his theory of salvation; (2) Lelio's paraphrase (1561) of 'archē' in John 1:1 as 'the beginning of the gospel' gave Fausto a hint in Biblical exegesis by help of which he constructed a new Christology. Apart from these suggestions, Fausto owed nothing to Lelio except a curiously far-fetched interpretation of John 8:58, and the stimulating remembrance of his pure character and brilliant gifts." In connection with his views on the Lord's Supper, *Opera* I, 423, Faustus makes a

passing reference to two writings of Laelius on the subject, one of which is, no doubt, the little tract contained in the appendix to Trechsel's, *Die Antitrinitarier vor Faustus Socinus,* Heidelberg, 1844, 438-444. Faustus appears, however, to owe more to Borrhaüs than to Laelius.

7. Gordon tells us (*The Sozzini and Their School, Theol. Review,* XVI, 298): "The country mansion of Scopeto, or 'The Bush,' six miles from the Porta Ovile, purchased in 1543 by the younger Mariano from the heirs of his cousin, Scipione Sozzini, remains very much in its original state." A rustic bench, formerly in the shade of a giant oak, is still displayed at the old estate. It was here that Faustus studied and indulged in the fancies common to all lads.

CHAPTER IV

THE FALLOW YEARS

THE death of his uncle left the young Faustus in something of a quandary. He must have leaned heavily upon the advice and encouragement of Laelius, and Przypkowski, his relative and biographer, frankly admits that he was during the ensuing years like a ship without a rudder. The remainder of 1562 was spent in visiting Italy and then Geneva, where he affiliated with the Italian congregation during the pastorate of Niccolo Balbani, whose son, Manfredo, became his warm friend and admirer. He finally returned to Lyons.

The year 1562 was also marked by the production of Socinus' first theological treatise, *An Explanation of the First Part of the First Chapter of John's Gospel*.[1] This booklet appeared anonymously and five years later was attributed to Laelius by Beza. In this little treatise, Faustus Socinus tackled one of the most difficult passages in the whole Bible, the very bulwark of the orthodox Trinitarian position. Taking up the first fifteen verses of the Gospel, line by line, Socinus argued that John was not declaring that

Christ was of one substance with the Father. In support of this view he urged the symbolism of the language and a careful exegesis of the text rather than an acceptance of traditional dogmas. The key-phrase, "And the Word was God," is thus interpreted: *Deus* or God (cf. Greek *Theos*) is not to be taken as a substantive but as an appellative, i. e., "the word was Divine," and parallels of this usage in the Old Testament, e. g. Moses' relation to Aaron (Exodus 4:16 cf. 7:1, etc.) are quoted.

A consideration of this first work of Socinus reveals the adumbration of one of his major positions, i. e., that Christ was divine, though not the Deity Himself; it also gives a clue to his strength and weakness as a controversialist. He clearly perceives the need of simpler categories for the Christian faith, and plainly states them, but he attempts to bolster these by an appeal to an infallible Scripture rather than to Christian experience or to the Bible interpreted in the light of historical criticism. The commentaries of Socinus are not wholly free from the faults of the age—special pleading, twisted exegesis, and an imperfect text.

In the year after the appearance of his first work (1563), Socinus returned to Italy and, to quote Przypkowski, "spent twelve whole years at the Court of Florence." The Polish biographer,

THE FALLOW YEARS

followed by Fock,[2] would imply that this time was spent in the service of the duke, Francesco de' Medici, but Gordon has conclusively shown from unpublished letters of Socinus that it was Isabella, the Duke's sister, who employed his services.[3] The larger part of this period seems to have been frittered away in abortive literary ventures and a desultory study of law which he did not finally abandon until 1567. Poetry always had a strong appeal for Socinus; he loved Dante, and having concluded his early work, *Concerning the Authority of Holy Scripture,* with an extensive quotation from the poet, he then gracefully turned it into the classic Latin mode. A true Italian, Socinus loved the sonnet and produced a number of fairly creditable examples which may be found in Ferentilli's collection and elsewhere.[4] In a letter written thirty years later to his friend Schmalz, Socinus warns the young man not to imitate him: "Who when I had already tasted of the springs of divine truth, was thus snatched away by certain other empty studies, so that I devoted the larger and more vigorous portion of my young manhood to inactivity and even ease."[5]

Perhaps it was the arrest of Paleario in 1567 that turned the young courtier from his literary and legal hobbies to a renewed consideration of religious problems. He had prudently refrained from preaching or publishing any religious work under his own name while at Florence, and had outwardly conformed to the Catholic Church before taking up his position at the Court. This course saved him from the persecution that had befallen his uncles, and preserved the friendship of Francesco, who protected his revenues long after he had left Italy.

In 1570, Socinus composed his most popular treatise, the little work *Concerning the Authority of Holy Scripture*. This book anticipated and no doubt influenced quite directly the popular defences of the credibility of the Bible, such as those of Lardner and other eighteenth century English writers, and even such a notable scholar as Grotius drew upon it in his *Concerning the Truth of the Christian Religion*.[6] There is little partisan bias in this book, a feature which made it acceptable to such widely differing groups as the Reformed Church in Basel (which commended the French version of 1592), and the Spanish Jesuits, one of whom, a certain Dominico Lopez, re-edited the work and published it under his own name (Seville, 1588). A Flemish version soon appeared, but no English translation was published until 1731.[7]

This little volume gives the fundamental ground for the Christian faith in the Bible, a doctrine that later became the basis for the Socinian system. It is interesting to note how the legal

THE FALLOW YEARS

background of the author keeps cropping out in his treatment of Scripture as a sort of Corpus Juris of the Christian faith. Socinus attempts to meet in turn the problems of the believer, the unbeliever, and the agnostic, and commences with a rather comprehensive consideration of the authenticity of the New Testament books. The case is well presented, and the critical arguments adduced in support of such books as the Gospel of Mark, are well chosen. As regards the books of disputed authorship, such as Hebrews and Revelation, Socinus shows no little scholarly acumen. Hebrews, he admits, is of doubtful Pauline authorship, but he takes care to emphasize its early date and its religious value. "I frankly confess," he says, "that it is doubted, not without cause, concerning this writing whether it was by that author to whom it is attributed by common consent."[8] The book of Revelation, he admits, has internal difficulties as to style and subject matter, but the external evidence convinces him that it was by the disciple whose name it bears.

One of the main theses of the work is that the historical basis of Scripture guarantees it as the medium for imparting Christian truth. Socinus selects the Sermon on the Mount as an ideal example of scriptural teaching, "in which," he declares, "nothing else is contained except the precepts for living as to who is able to be truly

FAUSTUS SOCINUS

blessed, and to be made worthy of heaven."[9]

Socinus' comparison and differentiation between the two Testaments to the advantage, of course, of the New, is also a note that is re-echoed in his later works.

Few scholars today would agree with Socinus that John is the primary source for the teaching and Luke for the history of Jesus, but this conclusion is, after all, the natural one for a scholar of an age which was uncritical as to the sources lying behind the present form of the books of the Bible.

Finally we find again and again repeated, Socinus' emphasis upon obedience to the ethical precepts of Christ as the great requirement of Christianity.[10]

The year after the composition of this work (1571) found Socinus in Rome, and perhaps this visit had an effect upon him not unlike that which Luther had experienced; at all events he left Italy for good four years later. He must have found the husband of Isabella de' Medici an uncongenial associate;[11] the impossibility of saying or publishing anything contrary to the teachings of the Catholic Church must have irked him; and, finally, his restless and idealistic nature must have been dissatisfied with the idle luxury of the Florentine court. There was no unpleasant break, or anything to suggest a flight, in Socinus' de-

THE FALLOW YEARS

parture. So long as Socinus refrained from publishing controversial works under his own name, the Duke was glad to forward the revenue accruing from the inheritance (one-fourth of the estate) that had been left to his grandson by Mariano, and repeatedly urged his friend to return. Socinus, on his part, faithfully kept his compact and until after the death of Francesco published no work under his own name that could have given offence, but he steadfastly refused to return to the Court of Tuscany.

There was something noble in this renunciation of a life of refined and pleasant associations. Even a hostile critic admits that "he condemned himself to run through the nations as an unfortunate vagabond." [12]

NOTES

1. *Explicatio Primae Partis Primi Capitis Evangelistae Johannis, Opera*, I., 75 ff.
2. *Der Socinianismus*, Kiel, 1847, 162
3. Article cit., *Encylopaedia Britannica*.
4. *Scelta di Stanze di Diversi Autori Toscanini*, 1579 (reprinted 1594). See also Cantu, *Gli Eretici d' Italia*, 1866, II., and the *Athenaeum*, August 11, 1877.
5. *Opera* I, 459^b.
6. The argument in Book III of the *De Veritate, Of the Authority of the Books of the New Testament*, is very similar to that of the *De Auctoritate*. Grotius, of course, is much more widely read than Socinus, and his allusions to ancient writers lend an added interest to his neat and balanced argument.
7. The *De Auctoritate Sanctae Scripturae*, (*Opera* I, 265ff.), is the only one of Socinus' works translated into English. The task was performed by Edward Coombe at the instigation of Bishop Smalbroke, who greatly admired this work of Socinus.
8. *Opera* I., 269^a. Socinus in his argument in this section anticipates the method of contemporary Higher Criticism.

FAUSTUS SOCINUS

9. *Opera* I., 277ᵇ.
10. See especially Chapter V, *Opera* I, 279-280.
11. He strangled the poor lady in the year following Socinus' departure (1572).
12. Guichard, op. cit., p. 378.

William Penn, the famous Quaker, was greatly moved by this renunciation. In his book, *Innocency with her Open Face* (1669), he says, Socinus, "being a young man, voluntarily did abandon the glories, pleasures, and honors of the great Duke of Tuscany's Court at Florence (that noted place for all worldly delicacies) and became a perpetual exile for his conscience." Penn went on to say that while he had never officially become a Socinian, and did not wish to be known as such, "if in anything I acknowledge the verity of his doctrine, it is for the truth's sake, of which in many things, he had a clearer prospect than most of his contemporaries." Wallace, *Antitrinitarian Biog.*, London, 1850, II, 325.

CHAPTER V

CONTROVERSY IN SWITZERLAND AND TRANSYLVANIA

NORTHERN Switzerland, the asylum of Italian Protestants, and the kindly host of Laelius Socinus, received his nephew cordially. Laelius had made many friends, and the memory of him was enough to give Faustus entrance into the most notable circles of the Reformed faith. The younger man was, moreover, not unknown, brief sojourns in Geneva and Zürich having served to introduce him personally.

Upon his arrival in 1574, Socinus found that during his twelve years at Florence, the religious situation in Switzerland had reached a new stage of development. Open war had, indeed, been finally abandoned by the hostile cantons, but the Protestant and Catholic groups were none the less active, and divided the country into two great armed camps. Calvin had died in 1564, and through the efforts of St. Francis de Sales, who had commenced a zealous propaganda of the old faith in the French-speaking districts, the wavering population south of Lake Geneva was kept Catholic. Bern, a strong Protestant canton, had

FAUSTUS SOCINUS

been compelled to surrender some of her recently acquired territory. Lucerne had become a strong center for the Counter Reformation, and in 1574, the Jesuits were established there. A special "Collegium Helveticum" had been founded at Milan for the training of young Swiss students for the priesthood. From his arch-episcopal see in the same city, the indefatigable Charles Borromeo conducted a well-directed counter offensive on behalf of Catholic Switzerland.

The result of the Counter Reformation in Switzerland was to stiffen Protestant resistance all along the line. Dogma assumed a position of supreme importance, and aberrations from the orthodox interpretation were dealt with severely. The great figures of the Swiss Reformation, many of whom had been as notable for their broad-mindedness as for their zeal, were dead. The generation that had known Bucer and Oecolampadius was passing away, and Bullinger, the warm friend of Laelius Socinus, had died in 1573. Italian refugees were especially suspect to this new orthodoxy. In 1563, the aged Ochino was brutally exiled in the bitter cold of a Swiss winter. In 1566, Valentino Gentile, a Neapolitan, was executed in Bern for heresy. A similar fate would no doubt have befallen Matteo Gribaldi of Padua in Geneva, but the Italian lawyer died while awaiting trial. Giovanni Paulo Alciati of Milan

SWITZERLAND AND TRANSYLVANIA

was forced to flee the country and take refuge in Poland. The particular tenets of these "heretics," to whose names we may add those of Paruta and Leonardi, differed considerably, but their common rock of offence was the orthodox doctrine of the Trinity. This is a significant fact when we realize that Faustus Socinus, arriving a trifle later upon the scene, found in the same doctrine one of his primary points of difference with the orthodox reformers.

Basel, termed by Przypkowski "the kindly hostess of the exiles of Christ," was chosen by Faustus as the seat of his labors. "The three solid years" Socinus spent here were occupied with careful study and continued controversy. He, first of all, made an investigation of the Scriptures and the few extant works of his uncle; he produced a poetical version of the Psalms; and several of his exegetical works appear to date from this period, although they were not published until much later. Faustus' health seems never to have been good, and often interrupted his studies; his increasing deafness also rendered conversation difficult.

Unlike Laelius, who had always advanced his views in the tentative fashion of a seeker after truth, Faustus had definite convictions and felt the urge to declare them. Many of his friends became estranged, but the fact that he refrained

FAUSTUS SOCINUS

from publishing any of his works probably accounts for his escape from Ochino's fate. A great point of discussion was the doctrine of the atonement. The traditional view of the propitiation of Christ on the Cross, as being an expiation made on behalf of man to conciliate the estranged majesty or implacable justice of God, was absolutely denied by Socinus. Jacques Couet (Covetus [1]), an able young theologian, was one of the principal defenders of the orthodox doctrine. Out of this controversy, which was carried on with great zeal, but in the best spirit, arose what is probably Socinus' greatest work—*Concerning Jesus Christ, the Saver*[2] (*De Jesu Christo Servatore*) in which he maintained that Christ's atoning work consisted in reconciling wayward men to a loving Father rather than in propitiating an offended Deity. Of course, the whole traditional hamartology and soteriology, with the insistence upon original sin, total depravity, and irresistible grace went by the board. The work is not incorrectly termed by Gordon "the great storehouse whence all the modern arguments against the medieval doctrine of Christ's satisfaction for sin has been drawn."[3] The Calvinists and even the Zwinglians were aroused. No wonder that the storm raged high and that Socinus felt his presence becoming increasingly unwelcome.

The final controversy at Basel was with a Florentine, Francisco Pucci [4] on the subject of the natural immortality of man. On June 4, 1577, Pucci issued a pamphlet entitled *Ten Arguments for the Immortality of Things, most especially of man in the First Creation*. It had been provoked by some contrary views of Socinus who immediately proceeded to reply to Pucci in a short treatise. Pucci issued a polite but determined defence, and was finally answered in a weighty and elaborate *Refutation* completed in Zürich, whither Socinus had retired early in 1578. The natural immortality of man, and the view that sin was the cause of natural death, were vigorously assailed by Socinus, for whom immortality was the reward of right conduct, and natural death a necessary physical event.[5]

Returning to Basel, Socinus put the finishing touches upon the *De Servatore* which was completed July 12, 1578, and immediately circulated in manuscript. It happened to catch the attention of Giorgio Biandrata whom Gordon aptly terms "an unscrupulous ecclesiastical wire-puller." Another of these disturbing Italians, Biandrata, was *persona non grata* in Reformed circles where he was accused not only of extreme left-wing opinions, but also of moral failures. He had, however, considerable influence in Poland and Transylvania because of his versatility and his medical skill.

FAUSTUS SOCINUS

During the rule of John Sigismund (1559-1571), and under the leadership of Biandrata and Francis David, anti-trinitarian views had permeated Transylvania. The celebrated disputation at Alba Julia (Weissenburg) in 1568, had resulted in the guarantee of full liberty of worship by the Diet to both Reformed and Unitarian churches. The latter were given the cathedral church of Cluj (Klausenburg), where David presided as bishop, and received control of many of the centers of education. The succession of the Bathori family to power proved a calamity for the liberals, the Jesuits were introduced, and Biandrata, a true Vicar of Bray, sought to curry favor with the dominant party by attacking David for opposing the invocation of Christ, and later by actually conforming to the Catholic Church. Now Socinus sincerely believed in the validity and efficacy (if not the necessity) of prayer to Christ, and Biandrata saw in him a convenient tool for the conversion or silencing of David; he therefore persuaded Socinus to go to Transylvania to win David over from his extreme position. To convert the sixty-eight-year-old David was no easy task, as Socinus soon found. A four-months' sojourn with David in Cluj (November 1578-February 1579) did not alter the old man's opinion. Socinus gave up the task as hopeless and proceeded to

SWITZERLAND AND TRANSYLVANIA

Poland which offered a more promising field for his labors.

Shortly after Socinus' departure, and at the instigation of Biandrata, David was tried upon a charge of "innovation" and condemned to imprisonment for life; late in the same year he died in the prison of Deva. Socinus cannot be said to have connived at the fate of his aged opponent and he decried the rage of Biandrata. However, he was willing that David should be prohibited from preaching, pending the verdict of the general synod, and he did not speak a brave word in defence of his aged host when it might have carried weight. Socinus, it is true, cannot be accused of violating David's hospitality, for he is careful to note in his correspondence that he was a "paying guest." [6] It would be wholly unfair to Socinus to trace a parallel between his attitude toward David and that of Calvin toward Servetus.

As for Biandrata, that unprincipled opportunist is said to have conformed to Catholicism in his wealthy old age and to have been secretly murdered by a greedy nephew who was impatient for the inheritance that was to be his.

NOTES

1. Bayle tells us (opus cit., V, 168-169, footnote), that Couet was a minister of Paris and was on his way to Frankfort, but that he had stopped at Socinus' lodgings *en route,* and had engaged in this controversy. That Couet was actually pastor of the French church

FAUSTUS SOCINUS

at this time, as a marginal note in the *Dictionnaire* suggests, appears to be extremely improbable. He seems to have been an enterprising post-graduate theological student who was introduced to Socinus by their friend, Manfredo Balbani.

2. The correct translation of *Servator* in this connection is a matter of some difficulty. The word is not a common one and Socinus was obviously avoiding the stock term *Salvator* because of its association with the traditional Soteriology. A careful check upon the usage of the word in the Classical, Vulgate, and later Latin give the two main meanings of *a personal representative* (cf. *Vicarius*) and *a deliverer* (cf. *Conservator*). While certain features of Socinus' Christology make the former rendering attractive, the latter is the more general and also the more germane to the subject of the work. It is, moreover, the Ciceronian usage. It has been decided, accordingly, to use the simple rendering *saver*. See Du Cange, *Glossarium*, Niort, 1886, VII, 442; Harper's *Latin Dictionary, Servator;* also the *Vulgate*, Prov. 24:12.

3. *Theological Review* XVI, 546.

4. Also a Protestant refugee in Switzerland. Many of his opinions were similar to those of Socinus. Venturing too far from his safe retreat he was seized and carried off to Rome where he was burnt. Socinus describes his travels in a letter to Dudicz, *Opera* I, 497. For a differing account of Pucci's death as the result of an accident, see Gordon, *Theological Review*, XVI, 55.

5. Socinus' argument is well summarized in the following quotation from the *Refutation, Opera* II, 274-275:

"For they who trust in God certainly die, but not on account of sin or by fate, but because of a human condition from the beginning of creation, and naturally."

6. "As for my living at his house, this was no free favor from him. In fact, I paid a very high board. This, indeed was later refunded to me by Biandrata: for he had invited me on these terms, that he should bear all the expense of my journey and stay in Transylvania." *Opera* II, 711.

CHAPTER VI

POLAND AND THE REFORMATION

POLAND, the field of Socinus' greatest labors and the scene of the last twenty-five years of his life, presented in the latter part of the sixteenth century an interesting and unique spectacle. If we except Russia, which remained a semi-oriental despotism despite the reforms of Ivan the Terrible, Poland became the largest European nation in the year 1569 when at the celebrated Diet of Lublin, the Grand Duchy of Lithuania, differing in both language and religion, was incorporated with Poland. The great nobles of both countries now composed the Diet which continued to elect the King and proceeded to define and extend its powers so as to render the monarch, except in time of war, little more than a figure-head with some appointive and administrative power. The famous *Pacta Conventa* embodying these articles limiting the royal power also provided for the free exercise of the Protestant faith.[1] The Duke of Anjou (later Henry III of France) was the first to be elected under the *Pacta Conventa* (1572), but upon his accession to the French throne he hastily and ignomini-

FAUSTUS SOCINUS

ously fled the country. The Poles, left in the lurch and deeply chagrined, elected a neighboring prince, Stephen Bathori of Transylvania, and he was crowned in 1575.

Despite her size and apparent unity, Poland could scarcely be termed a nation in the sense in which England, France, and Spain had developed into national states. In neither Italy nor Germany, it is true, had a strong central government appeared, but whereas foreign domination and a multiplicity of independent units hindered its rise in those countries, in Poland the persistence of a peculiar form of the feudal system, rooted in the social and economic soil of the country, militated against the rise of a truly national state. Throughout the fifteenth and sixteenth centuries, along with the growth of the cities, a powerful and patriotic middle class had arisen in nearly all the European countries; Poland remained relatively unaffected by this general movement. In Danzig, Posen, and other commercial cities on the western border, business was in the hands of the large German population and a sprinkling of Scottish and Jewish merchants. Krakow remained a cultural rather than a commercial center, and trade in the scattered cities of Galicia and Lithuania was almost wholly in the hands of the Jews, who in some towns comprised nearly half of the population. Even the rural poulation was non-Polish

POLAND AND THE REFORMATION

in large areas—Lithuanians, Livonians, and White Russians to the north and east, Ukrainians, the autonomous hordes of Cossacks and Red Russians to the southeast. These peoples were attached to Poland chiefly because the local nobility preferred its loose hegemony to the more exacting demands of neighboring states. The rural areas whether agricultural, pasture, woodland, or simply waste, were divided into vast numbers of small estates governed by the numerous but poor nobility (the *szlachta*) who comprised about one-tenth of the total population. The terms "land-owner" and "noble" were practically interchangeable and even the descendant of a land-owning noble was considered to be of noble rank. The small size of the estates, coupled with the predominantly military interest of the nobility, retarded any real advance in agriculture, and the average aristocratic landlord was much more interested in raising horses for his military equipage than grain or cattle. So small were many of the estates that it was a byword that the dog of a poor noble, though he sat in the middle of his owner's estate, would have his tail across the boundary of a neighbor's fief. The peasantry who worked these estates were very poor and illiterate; virtually they were serfs. In former times there had been a sturdy yeoman class above the level of the serf, as in England, but these *kmieci* had almost entirely disappeared at the close of the sixteenth century.[2]

During the latter half of the sixteenth century, Poland, or rather her numerous aristocracy, experienced a belated Renaissance. While zealous to retain the national dress and many of the old customs, the Polish nobility eagerly welcomed the study of classic literature and art. Krakow was the great seat of this flowering of culture, and her enlarged curriculum catered to the needs of hundreds of students. Copernicus, a graduate of Krakow, while primarily a man of science, was greatly interested in the art and letters of North Italy, and may have done much to stimulate a wide-spread acquaintance with the new cultural movement which swept over Poland in the generation that followed him.

Along with the classical and artistic movement came a great awakening in the national literature —an awakening that went hand in hand with the growth of Protestantism. Martin Bielski (1495-1570), whose *Kronika Polska* was the first history of Poland in the vernacular, was a Protestant. The first national poet of any prominence, Nicholas Rej of Naglowice (1505-1569) was another. John Seklucyan (d. 1578), who made the first Polish version of the New Testament, was a Lutheran divine. In fact, a whole series of Protest-

POLAND AND THE REFORMATION

ant translations of the Bible appeared and enjoyed a wide circulation.

The soil had been prepared for Protestantism for a century preceding the Reformation by the labors of Hussite missionaries from Bohemia. This Hussite propaganda was rendered all the more easy by the close affinity between the Czech and Polish languages and the practically local autonomy of the Polish nobles. Despite persecutions such as that which took place in Posen in 1439, when five Hussite pastors were burnt in the market-place, the movement grew apace and by 1500 there were nearly two hundred Hussite houses of worship many of which were under the protection of the nobility.[3]

The Lutheran movement, so strong in near-by Saxony, soon made its power felt in Great Poland, where it sung and preached its way into favor with large numbers. As early as 1530 Lutheran hymns were being sung in Thorn, and Danzig became a strong center of missionary propaganda. Seklucyan, who was personally acquainted with Luther, was one of the foremost leaders in this movement, and his Polish translations of the Scriptures and Protestant hymns were published and widely circulated. Cruciger and other Lutheran divines also made extensive preaching tours with much success. Livonia, with its strong German population, became largely Lutheran af-

FAUSTUS SOCINUS

ter the conversion of the Teutonic Order to the Reformation, and remains so until this day, while other forms of Protestantism have practically disappeared in Poland, except for the recent German settlers.

Whereas the Lutherans had found their most fertile fields in Great Poland [4] and Livonia, the Reformed doctrines emanating from Switzerland found a ready welcome, at a somewhat later date, in Little Poland and in scattered points to the East. The Swiss reformers found powerful patrons in the Radziwills, who had embraced Reformed opinions and who were in active correspondence with Calvin.[5] The leading spirit in the Polish Reformed Church was the noble John Laski, who had been won over to the Reformation by Zwingli, and who enjoyed a great reputation outside his own country as a scholar and preacher. The Lutherans, however, did not approve of Laski's efforts on behalf of the Reformed Church in Germany, and he was glad to accept the call to be overseer of the foreign Protestant churches and schools in London (1548). The accession of Mary to the English throne and her persecution of the Protestants forced Laski and his flock to seek safety in flight. The vessel bearing the 175 refugees was wrecked and Laski and his followers received the harshest treatment from Danish and German Lutherans. Not until they reached Dan-

POLAND AND THE REFORMATION

zig did the unhappy refugees find a haven of hospitality. Laski himself spent a couple of years in Germany seeking to reconcile the Reformed and Lutheran bodies, but being unsuccessful and seeing the way clear for his return to Poland, he hastened back to his native land (1556). Ably seconded by Lutomirski and Sarnicki, Laski did much to promote the advancement of the Reformed faith in the cities of the north and most notably in Little Poland. Lutomirski, who is termed by Wotschke "the first preacher of consequence and influence in Little Poland,"[6] exercised an important ministry in that section. Laski had been rejoiced by the union of the Bohemian Brethren with the Reformed in 1555 and unsuccessfully attempted to effect a *rapprochement* with the Lutherans. He enjoyed the unbounded confidence of Calvin who frequently corresponded with him, and who regarded his untimely death in 1660 as a great blow to the progress of the Reformed faith in Poland.

The first general synod of the Reformed Church held at Pinczow in 1555 had shown a wide diversity of opinion in that body, and after the death of Laski, who had been the great unifying force, the cleavage became all the more apparent. While the union of the Reformed and the Brethren had been highly successful, there were two other groups that chafed under the Genevan dis-

FAUSTUS SOCINUS

cipline, the Anabaptists, who had received a considerable impetus from the recent labors of Menno, and who were represented by a vigorous leader in Czechowitz, and a growing Antitrinitarian group led by men like Lismanini, Goniodski, Biandrata, and Stancaro. To this latter group, which became the nucleus for the widespread Antitrinitarian movement headed by Faustus Socinus, we must now turn for a more detailed consideration.

NOTES

1. The unfortunate *liberum veto* by which any member of the Diet could nullify any action, and even dissolve the Diet itself, by pronouncing the dread word: *Niepozwalam,* was never exercised by a single member until the well-known case of the Lithuanian "nuntius," Sicinski, in 1652. It was afterwards employed with paralyzing effect until its abolition in 1791. It failed, however, in 1658 to stay the suppression of the Socinians. See Wilbur, *Our Unitarian Heritage,* The Beacon Press, Inc., Boston, 1925, 175.

2. A hundred years later when the condition of the peasantry had not greatly changed, Connor, the British physician of John Sobieski, published his *Letters on Poland,* which vividly describe their unfortunate condition.

3. See Reid's note in Mosheim, *Century XVI,* Chapter 2, Sec. 23. Some of the oldest memorials of the Polish vernacular literature appear to date from this movement. There is a fragment of a hymn in honor of Wyclif, and even the celebrated *Hymn to the Virgin* may have a Hussite basis.

4. It must be remarked, however, that the Bohemian Brethren also had a large following in Great Poland, and that there was a strong Reformed congregation at Posen under the devoted leadership of its chief elder, George Israel.

5. Wotschke in his *Der Briefwechsel der Schweizer mit den Polen (Archiv. für Reform. Gesch.),* Leipzig, 1908, lists 527 letters exchanged between the Protestants of Switzerland and Poland and gives many of them entire.

6. See his interesting monograph on Lutomirski, *Archiv. für Reform. Gesch.,* III Jahrgang (1905-1906), 105-171.

CHAPTER VII

THE RISE OF ANTITRINITARIANISM IN POLAND

THE Unitarian movement in Poland had its genesis in a cultured Catholic aristocracy rather than in the middle classes of the cities or in the country gentry where Protestantism had its strongest support. In this respect it followed the line already taken in Italy, and we find in Poland many Italian religious radicals who were refugees from their own states or from orthodox Protestant countries that had formerly sheltered them.

Krakow, the seat of learning, was not unnaturally the birthplace of the movement in Poland. The court was there, and Sigismund Augustus and his Italian queen, Bona Sforza, made a hobby of patronizing new ideas. The king had some friendly correspondence with Calvin on the subject of reforming the Polish church, and the queen was an admirer of Ochino. One of the most influential persons at court was the Italian, Francesco Lismanini, head of the Franciscan order in Poland and confessor to the Queen. It was he who first made the king acquainted with the writings of Calvin, and who was later sent to Switzerland to investigate the actual practice of the Reformed churches with instructions to report his findings to the king. Lismanini was the leader of a small group of liberal Catholic scholars which met privately for the discussion of the new opinions, and which received Laelius Socinus with open arms when he made his first Polish visit in 1551; the fact that Laelius stopped at the house of Lismanini may account in part for the subsequent theological position of his host. It would be a mistake to assume, as some writers have carelessly done, that Laelius exerted any considerable effect upon the progress or ideology of the Antitrinitarian movement in Poland during his short visits there; he had probably more to learn from Lismanini and the rest than to teach.[1]

All the disaffected elements now seized the occasion for an open attack upon the Catholic Church. The Diets of 1550 and 1552 attacked the abuses and obscurantism so rife in Polish Catholicism and showed a friendly front to the reformers. The left-wing group of the Protestants, later to assume leadership in the Unitarian movement, openly denounced the Roman Church. Francesco Stancaro, an Italian and Professor of Hebrew at Krakow, was especially outspoken, and at his behest a monastery at Pinczow was purged of both monks and images and a church on the Reformed

ANTITRINITARIANISM IN POLAND

model organized on the spot. Shortly after, (1555), the first Protestant synod was held in the town, and the movement spread like wildfire over Little Poland. Gregory Pawel, another scholar of repute, a native Pole, became head of a flourishing congregation in Krakow. Peter Goniodzki (Gonesius) who had gone abroad to study for the priesthood but had been won over to the Protestants, returned to Poland imbued with anabaptist and anti-trinitarian ideas. He became pastor of a Reformed congregation, and at the Synod of Secemin in 1556 refused to give his assent to any creed save the Apostles', and openly attacked the doctrine of the Trinity. Goniodzki found a powerful patron in the Lithuanian magnate, John Kiszka, himself something of a scholar, who made him pastor of a church at Wegrow, and founded some score of churches, all of which under the leadership of Goniodzki, Budny, and others became Antitrinitarian.[2]

Foreign religious refugees began to flock into Poland and swelled the number of the radicals in the ranks of the Reformed. Biandrata arrived in 1558, accompanied by Alciati, and the same year witnessed visits by Gentile and Laelius Socinus. In the following year, Pierre Stator, a Frenchman, arrived in Poland and became rector of the Pinczow school at the synod of Pinczow in 1561, he too took an avowedly Unitarian position.

FAUSTUS SOCINUS

Relations between the orthodox group with which Calvin maintained a lively correspondence, and the restive radicals became more and more strained. Laski in the right wing and Lismanini in the left used their best offices to prevent an open rupture, but unsuccessfully. Lismanini had, moreover, lost the royal favor which he had formerly enjoyed,[3] as well as his early position of leadership in the reforming movement. In the midst of a warm debate at the Synod of Krakow (1562), he cried: "Let all the Doctors leave me one God, and not divide Him; they may have a mediator such as they have devised for themselves."[4] He was shortly after exiled and is said to have committed suicide in a fit of despair at Königsberg in 1563.

The death of Lismanini following that of Laski destroyed all hopes for a reconciliation between the orthodox and radicals in the Reformed Church, and in 1565 the Antitrinitarians, having been forced to secede, at a conclave in Piotrkow, met in a separate synod at Wegrow.

The new church was born amid difficulties; royal edicts (1564-1566) deprived it at the outset of many of its leaders—men like Alciati, Gentile, and Biandrata, who were forced to leave the country. More serious than the persecution by the state and the Catholic Church, and the opposition shown by the Lutheran and Reformed bodies, were the internal dissensions that weakened the new movement. Indeed, but for the protection afforded by individual nobles and certain communities, the radicals would have been exterminated as they had been elsewhere in Europe with the exception of Transylvania.

There were certain general positions held by these early Unitarians, who were at first more generally known by the name of Anabaptist, or the Minor Church and later as the Polish Brethren. All denied the orthodox doctrine of the Trinity and assigned a subordinate position to the Son; after the Synod of Wegrow (1565) infant baptism was rejected and all adult converts required to undergo re-baptism. There was a wide divergence of opinion upon the doctrine of the Person of Christ, and we may say that prior to the advent of Faustus Socinus in 1579 there were three main divisions in the Church upon this point.

The largest group, which took its name from its patron, Stanislaus Farnowski (Farnovius), and its Christology in large part from Goniodzki, held an Arian view of Christ and had a strong Anabaptist strain. There was a large number of really able scholars in this group, the Poles, Wisnowski, Niemojewski, and Czechowitz with whom Faustus Socinus had many a friendly but acute controversy, and the German, Schomann, who appears to have produced the lucid and concise little Catechism of Krakow in 1574—the first Unitarian Confession of Faith.[5]

There was also a left-wing group which had its chief strength in Lithuania and whose members were termed Budnaeans from their founder, Simon Budny; they opposed to the more conservative Christology of the Farnovians a purely Ebionite conception, maintaining that Christ was no more than man distinguishable from the rest of humanity by his moral character and special commission as an ambassador of God. It is possible that this group, which had its greatest hold in the eastern borders of the Polish state, was influenced and augmented by refugees of that sect of Judaizing Christians which had arisen in Great Russia in the previous century and had been sternly repressed after making considerable headway.[6] Faustus Socinus had many controversies with the Budnaeans, especially with Christian Francken and Jacobus Palaeologus. The later Socinians always referred to this group as the semi-Judaizers, and its connection with the views of David is evident.[7] In 1570, an excellent translation of the Scriptures into Polish was produced by Budny and published at Nieswiez;[8] it became the standard for the Unitarians, just as the earlier version published under the patronage of Nicho-

ANTITRINITARIANISM IN POLAND

las Radziwill (1553) was the authorized translation for the Reformed Church.

A group, mediating between the Farnovians and the Budnaeans, which anticipated in a rough way the later position of Faustus Socinus, was headed by Pierre Stator and Gregory Pawel. This group was known as the Pinczovians, from the town of Pinczow where their principal school was located.

The death of Stancaro in 1574 and the expulsion of many of the early leaders had deprived the Unitarians of organized unity. Only the patronage of nobles like Kiszka, John Sieninski and Andrew Dudicz enabled the Church to maintain its existence. Sieninski, who had built a new town at Rakow in 1569, welcomed a group of Pinczovians, who founded not only a church but also the famous school at that place; and Dudicz, formerly a bishop of the Catholic Church in Hungary, a man respected for his character and learning, afforded the Unitarians an asylum at his town of Szmigiel (Schmiegel) in Great Poland. Here a strong church was established.

NOTES

1. See Trechsel, Op. cit., 156.
2. The power of the nobility is shown by the fact that when in 1592, a member of the Reformed Church succeeded to the estates of Kiszka, all these churches became Reformed with their new patron.
3. On his tour of the Protestant centers, which included a visit to Calvin at Geneva, Lismanini had married and had openly broken with the Roman Church. Sigismund Augustus, who for reasons of state

FAUSTUS SOCINUS

was unwilling to espouse openly the Protestant cause, felt this action to be indiscreet, and it took the combined influence of Lutherans like Cruciger and Calvinists like Laski to secure the readmission of Lismanini to an active rôle in the Polish Reformation.

4. See, *Epitome of the History of the Origin of the Unitarians in Poland*, John Stoinski appended to Sand, p. 183. (*Bibliotheca Anti-Trinitariorum*, Freistadt, 1684).

5. A long and interesting note in Reid's edition of Mosheim, *Century XVI*, Sec. III, Part II, Ch. IV:10, (Note 2), contains a lengthy abstract of this important work.

Farnowski after his secession from the main body founded a school and a church at Sandec. His works were written for the most part in Polish. Farnowski seems to have lived to a ripe old age, for he is mentioned as collaborating with the faithful Wisnowski upon a theological work in 1614. Schmalz's efforts to win Farnowski back to the main body after the death of Socinus were unavailing. For the life of this interesting reformer, see Bock, *Historia Anti-Trinitariorum*, Königsberg and Leipzig, 1776, I (1), 334 ff.

6. See the *Jewish Encylopaedia*, New York, 1902, VII, 369-370.

7. Budny was on friendly terms with several Jewish scholars, notably Hezekiah David Abulafia who mentions the high regard in which he held the Talmud. He may also have been influenced by the great rabbi, Isaac ben Abraham Troki whose anti-Christian polemic, the *Hizzuk Emunah*, is still widely read in Jewish circles. It was perhaps these Jewish contacts as much as Budny's actual opinions that led to the designation "Semi-Judaisers" which Socinians found convenient as a label to differentiate these radicals from themselves. See the *Jewish Encylopaedia*, III, 421.

8. The little pamphlet appended to Sand's *Bibliotheca, Concerning the Unitarian Presses in Poland and Lithuania*, p. 201, declares that this work was published at Zaslaw by Matthias Kawieczynski.

CHAPTER VIII

SOCINUS IN POLAND

STEPHEN Bathori's joint hegemony over Transylvania and Poland made the latter country of easy access to Socinus, who arrived in Krakow in the latter part of 1579. The Italian had anticipated a cordial reception in this land where greater freedom of conscience was permitted than in any other, but no such welcome awaited him. Catholics and orthodox Protestants already regarded him as a dangerous innovator, and even the disunited Unitarian group refused to admit him to its fellowship. The Polish Antitrinitarians maintained that adult baptism was essential and Socinus, while himself no stickler on the subject of the sacraments, refused to be rebaptized and remained outside the fellowship of the church, although he strongly supported the movement.

Socinus was now, at forty years of age, in the very prime of life, and he settled down with zeal in Krakow to advance and defend his views against all comers. Among the Antitrinitarians he found his most congenial allies in the scholars of Pinczow and Rakow. The other groups fre-

FAUSTUS SOCINUS

quently opposed him. The Farnovians, who maintained the pre-existence of the person of Christ, were repelled by what they considered to be the Ebionite view of Socinus [1]; the Budnaeans, on the other hand, were incensed at the outcome of the controversy with David, and considered Socinus' defence of the invocation of Christ as a concession to superstition.

More acrimonious were the debates with Reformed or Catholic scholars. A certain Andrew Wolan, one of the Reformed group, charged Socinus and the other Unitarians with being Ebionites or Samosatenes,[2] and provoked a lengthy reply. Socinus' chief work on the person of Christ, *Concerning the Nature of Christ*, forms a valuable supplement to the *Concerning the Saver*, which had dealt exclusively with the Work of Christ. Deliberately avoiding the ground covered in his earlier work, Socinus drew a sharp distinction between the Person of God and the Person of Christ. He thus summarizes his position in the beginning of the first part of his *Response:* "We believe in, and adore one God, the father of all, without beginning and origin, and one lord, the son of God, the man Jesus of Nazareth, crucified and resurrected." [3]

It was not long before Socinus found a more redoubtable opponent in Jacobus Palaeologus.[4] Disclaiming responsibility for the inception of the

SOCINUS IN POLAND

controversy, and paying tribute to the learning and eloquence of his opponent, Socinus proceeded to the exposition of one of his most learned and revolutionary treatises, *The Defence of the True Opinion of the Political Magistracy*,[5] in which he defined his views concerning the Civil Authority, Law, and War. Socinus' legal background appears to have stood him in good stead, but one wonders what his learned ancestors would have said of some of his ideas. In the First Part, Palaeologus' ridiculous statement that Christ was a "lamb" before his exaltation, but after it a "lion," was refuted; Socinus maintained that the character of Christ was at all times consistent, and that His exaltation only increased his capacity for gentleness and forgiveness. If Jesus is the Prince of Peace, argued Socinus, his followers are prohibited from waging war under any condition.[6]

The whole question of obedience to the civil power, and the right of Christians to hold public office, is then treated at length. Capital punishment is denounced as contrary to the precepts of Christ, who taught us to love our enemies. Despite the dogma of the Divine Right of Kings then taking form, Socinus declared that human legislation was from God, in so far only as it accorded with the revealed will of God (New Testament standards). Socinus also held that no Christian could exercise the office of magistrate if his func-

FAUSTUS SOCINUS

tions included the infliction of the death penalty.[7]

Shortly after the tilt with Palaeologus, and while the long drawn-out controversy with Wolan continued, the Jesuit College of Posen issued a series of *Assertions concerning the Three and One God against the new Samosatenians*. These *Assertions* Socinus answered briefly, *seriatim*. His position can be summarized as follows: God, the Father, is One and Indivisible; the man, Jesus Christ, is God's Son, exercising divine functions, but not a person of the Godhead; the Holy Spirit, as he finely observes,[8] is God immanent in our lives. God Himself is Spirit; to postulate a separate person in the Godhead is superfluous.

These controversies succeed in gaining Socinus the goodwill of the majority of the Unitarians, especially the scholarly group at Rakow with which he had made common cause, but they also drew down upon him the active hostility of other Protestants and of the Catholics. His theological opponents were not slow in seizing upon the *De Magistratu* as a piece of "seditious" literature, and presented it as such to the king. Stephen Bathori was, however, too busy with his Livonian campaigns and his plans for the new University of Vilna to persecute an Italian refugee, and Socinus experienced no official opposition in his reign. When Stephen died in 1586 a storm of

SOCINUS IN POLAND

Civil disorder augmented the religious strife. A violent election in which blood was shed and a rival candidate, Maximilian of Austria, was driven from the country by force, finally resulted in the selection of a Swedish prince, Sigismund Augustus, as king. Despite his nationality, Sigismund was a devout Catholic, but he did not feel strong enough to persecute the Protestants— even the Unitarians, for many years.

Troubled by these disturbances, and wearied by the storm of ecclesiastical strife in Krakow, Socinus was glad to remain at Pawlikowice, the neighboring estate of a friendly nobleman, Christopher Morsztyn. From this point Socinus could keep in close touch with affairs in the city and the country at large, and at the same time have leisure to pursue his theological studies. The Jesuits at Posen had not let their *Assertions* stand refuted, and one of their number, Gabriel Eutropius, returned to the attack. Elaborating upon his previous tabulated reply, Socinus produced a fuller *Defence,* in which his former criticism of the Dogma of the Trinity was expressed at greater length and his own position clarified.

For a dozen years and more Socinus' constant travel and the insecurity of his standing had perhaps prevented him from seriously contemplating marriage, but now in the happy family circle of the Morsztyns, he found a noble wife in Elizabeth, a daughter of his host. Despite Socinus' forty-seven years the marriage seems to have been a true love-match. The following year was blest by the arrival of a little daughter, who was named Agnes in honor of her paternal grandmother.[9] To the great grief of Socinus his beloved wife died in September of the same year. He became dangerously ill, and to cap this misfortune, his faithful patron, the Grand Duke Francesco of Tuscany, died and a long series of difficulties regarding his Italian revenues commenced.[10]

Upon recovering from his illness, Socinus returned to Krakow in the fall of the same year (1587) and threw himself whole-heartedly into the work of the churches, which had been seriously impaired by the growing opposition from without and the distracting divisions within. We have already noted how the Unitarians were split into three distinct factions—the followers of Budny who had been weakened by the deposition of their leader in 1584, the Farnovians or Arians, and the Pinczovians, the moderate party. In the year 1588, at Brest-Litowsk, far away on the border of Lithuania, the disunited church met in an epoch-making synod. The moderates saw in Socinus a leader who commanded universal respect, and whose nationality freed him from the family jealousies so rife in Polish affairs. They were pleased by the success with which Socinus

SOCINUS IN POLAND

confuted the trouble-making Budnaeans at the Synod, and the result was that Peter Stoinski,[11] the son of Stator and his successor as leader of the Pinczovians, became a devoted admirer and follower of Socinus, and succeeded in uniting the Pinczovians with Socinus' own growing personal following among the Racovians and others. Many of the Farnovians were also won over to the coalition which now presented a unified front to its opponents and later became known as Socinian.

In the following year at the Synod of Lublin another controversy, with a certain Nicholas Zitinski, only added to Socinus' established reputation. Stoinski's influence and eloquence again had much to do with the strengthening of Socinus' leadership. In the fall of the same year Socinus' sensible refutation of the Chiliasts at the Synod of Chmielnik, although conducted by correspondence, won him the adherence of more of the middle-of-the-road men.

The unfortunate disposal of his Italian property, finally lost by the action of the holy office in Siena (October 1590) which disinherited him, freed Socinus from the obligation to publish only anonymously, if at all. The result was the publication of several works, including the famous *Concerning the Saver*. Socinus' reputation grew apace; he maintained his position of leadership in Poland by frequent journeyings and a con-

FAUSTUS SOCINUS

stant correspondence from his home base at Krakow.

Not only Poland, but also Transylvania, experienced a great increase in the power and influence of the Unitarians, and while the church in the latter principality had its own superintendents, the advice and leadership of Socinus was constantly sought. Radecki, Spangenberg, and Enyedi, three of the leaders of the Transylvanians, maintained an extensive correspondence with Socinus at Krakow and the influence of the followers of David, or Semi-Judaizers as their opponents termed them, was greatly diminished. Spangenberg, a native of Antwerp, left Cluj (Klausenburg) to teach at Rakow, and Erasmus Jansen, on the other hand, left Poland for a professor's chair at Cluj. The two churches maintained a close *rapport*, and both increasingly acknowledged the leadership of the Sienese reformer.

NOTES

1. Socinus' most redoubtable opponent among the Farnovians was a certain Erasmus Jansen with whom in 1584 he had a controversy on the pre-existence of Christ. This disputation may be found in the *Opera* II, 489ff. The tone of this controversy was friendly, and Erasmus was later admitted to the Socinian faculty at Cluj on condition that he would not teach the pre-existence of Christ.

2. That there was considerable truth in these "charges" cannot be denied. The Ebionites, a sect of the primitive church that was confined largely to Jewish Christians, maintained the strictly human character of the person of Christ. Paul of Samosata, bishop of Antioch in the middle of the third century, held a similar view. The chief difference between the Ebionites and Paul was in their respec-

tive backgrounds—Judaism accounting for the Ebionite view, and the Logos Philosophy for Paul's. Both denied the personal pre-existence of Christ.

3. *De Jesu Christi, Filii dei Natura Sive Essentia, Opera* II, 375ª.

4. This Palaeologus was a member of the ancient family of Byzantine emperors, and a native of Chios. Seized in Rome on a charge of heresy, he succeeded in escaping to Germany. His erudition, his pleasing manners, and his noble family served in Protestant lands, at least, to protect him, like Socinus, from active persecution. He allied himself to the extreme Budnaean group in Poland, and his reputation secured him the rectorship of the Unitarian school at Cluj. He was seized, however, by order of the Emperor Maximilian, when journeying through Moravia, and transmitted to Rome where he was burnt in 1585. For notices on this interesting character, see Bock, op. cit., 583-587, Wallace, *Antitrinitarian Biography*, London, 1850, 266-271.

5. *Contra Palaeologum, Defensio Verae Sententiae De Magistratu Politico., Opera* II, 1 ff.

6. Socinus explicitly declared "there is no war so just that Christian men following the example of Christ could or ought to plunge into the waging of war." *Opera* II, 8-9.

7. Although the views expressed in this work were a source of considerable embarrassment to the later Socinians, they remained remarkably loyal to them. Cf. Wolzogen *Annotationes ad Quattuor Quaestiones de Magistratu et Bello*, 1656.

8. "It is said that God dwells in us, or abides in us, because of the fact that he gives us of his spirit—God Himself is spirit, etc." Remarks on *Assertiones Theologicae de Trino et Uno Deo, adversus novos Samosatenicos. Opera* II, 429ᵇ.

9. Agnes Sozzini was brought up on her grandfather's estate, but her father, whether in Krakow or farther afield, kept himself informed of her welfare. A letter to a friend under date of August 9, 1595, voices his solicitude for her (*Opera* I, 473ª).

Although only a young girl at the time of her father's death, Agnes always remained true to his principles, and not long after married a Unitarian nobleman, Stanislaus Wiszowaty. Their son, Andrew, became a leader in the church, a devoted pastor and a learned scholar. Agnes Wiszowaty died at the home of her son in Robkow, January 20, 1654.

10. Socinus' troubled state of mind is revealed in a letter written to his friend, John Balkerowski, (November 21, 1587), in which he mentions his great grief at the loss of his wife, his anxiety over the political situation, his own poor state of health, and his desire to meet with a certain Gedanus. (*Opera* I, 426).

11. He had taken this Polish surname upon his entrance into the Polish nobility.

CHAPTER IX

CONFLICT AND CONSUMMATION

SOCINUS had never coveted the reputation of a heresiarch,[1] nor did he have the thirst for martyrdom common to so many of the radicals of Reformation and post-Reformation movements. He always considered himself a moderate, and simply a clarifier of the obscured truths of the New Testament. Extremists such as Atheists, Anabaptists, Chiliasts, and Semi-Judaizers were distasteful to him, and he combated them with voice and pen at synods and in disputations.[2] Socinus appears never to have realized the revolutionary implications of his ideas as did some of his followers and more especially some of his opponents.

The smouldering hostility to Socinus in Krakow, which had been somewhat allayed by his departure in 1586, never burst into flame. The reformer had realized the danger of his position, and in a beautiful letter to his friend, Dudicz, he had discussed the possibility of martyrdom. "I do not imagine," he wrote, "that you have told me to be possessed by the desire for death, but I may say this much, if it seems best to God that I should suffer death for His divine truth, I would consider it as a great favor to myself, that he should render me in some degree comparable not only to so many others who loved Him, but even to His own dearest Son, my Lord." [3]

Socinus' return to the city proper and his active participation in the work of the church rekindled the latent fires of opposition. The Jesuits,[4] who bore no good-will to Socinus since his able disputations with their brethren at Posen, were especially incensed at the growing power of this heretic and his followers. They maintained that heretical works, especially the *Concerning the Saver* with its blasphemies against the Holy Mass, were being widely circulated, that students in the University, and, worse still, some of the professors were being won over to these pernicious doctrines. They felt that it was a blight upon an episcopal city that was expending such care on rebuilding its famous cathedral to tolerate the presence of an arch-heretic who would have been expelled or even executed in any other country.

Socinus' powerful patrons and personal following prevented any organized acts of violence upon his person or property, but in 1594, the reformer, now prematurely old and feeble, was assaulted in the street by a brutal trooper, evidently in the pay of his enemies. Fortunately he came

FAUSTUS SOCINUS

through the encounter without serious injury.

The beginning of the year 1598 found Socinus ill and confined to his lodgings. His literary activity was, however, increasing, and a work, *Against the Atheists,* on which he had spent great pains, was finally completed.

On Ascension Day, when Socinus was still confined to his bed by illness, a fanatical mob of students from the University, at the instigation of the Catholic authorities, burst into the house, plundered its furnishings, and seized his manuscripts, books, and papers. The sick man was dragged half-naked from his bed, and an impromptu parade was begun to the famous old Ring-Platz in the heart of the city. Arriving there, the mob lighted a bonfire, and the confiscated literature was applied to the blaze, Socinus being warned that he would go the way of his books if he did not recant. Despite his years, ill-health, and harsh treatment, the lone martyr refused to be cowed even when a drawn sword was brandished over his head. "I do not recant," he stoutly declared. "Where I have stood, I stand and will stand through the grace of our Lord Jesus Christ until my last breath. Do what God allows you to do!"

Threats being of no avail, it was resolved to throw the obstinate heretic into the river, and dragging its victim along, the procession made its

CONFLICT AND CONSUMMATION

way south towards the Vistula. The clamor of the boisterous students attracted the attention of one of the professors, Martin Wadowitz, whose residence faced the street through which they were passing. He leaned out of the window and asked what was the matter. "We are leading the Heresiarch," came the response. Moved by pity or curiosity the professor contrived to have the unhappy victim admitted and locked the door on the students, when to his surprise he found that he had saved the life of a good friend.[5]

While the authorities ecclesiastical and civil had connived at the violence of the students, they had no authority to arrest Socinus, as the Act of Toleration of Wola (1573) was still in force. Opinion at the university was divided. Many of the professors bitterly assailed Wadowitz for his humane and courageous action, but the rector, Lelowitz, and others supported him.[6] When he had recuperated sufficiently, the sick and weary reformer slipped away quietly from the home of his benefactor and escaped to the country.

A pleasant retreat was found at Luslawice, thirty miles to the south-east of Krakow, and here Socinus stayed for the five or six remaining years of his life. His good host, Adam Blonski, did everything possible to render his guest's sojourn comfortable and pleasant. Though he mourned the loss of his precious papers, especially the

FAUSTUS SOCINUS

Against the Atheists which he considered his ablest work, Socinus did not cease from his literary activity. Several Catechisms appeared, which formed a basis for the famous *Racovian Catechism* produced by Schmalz and Moskorzewski a year after his death (1605).[7] For some time Socinus had been urged by a friendly "Evangelical" or Protestant of the orthodox persuasion to write a tractate on the reasons for the alleged superiority of the Socinian faith. Socinus' answer was a short and often neglected treatise—perhaps its overpowering title has scared away prospective readers.[8]

Paying tribute to the "solid piety" of the "Evangelicals," Socinus makes the same general criticism of them that liberal Protestants since that time have always made of their conservative brethren. The first critique is ethical: Socinus attacks the view that the ethical teaching of the Bible is consistent throughout. The thesis: "The precepts of Christ pertaining to morals do not differ from those handed down by Moses" is criticized and Socinus cites the difference adduced by Christ Himself between the law of retribution and the law of forgiving love, as shown in Matthew 5:21 ff. The second criticism is more detailed and theological in character, and in brief is that the "Evangelicals" had uncritically carried over from the Catholic Church a whole series of misconceptions regarding the sacraments and various doctrines, especially that of the atonement. This little work, finished in July, 1599, is the last important dated work that we have from the pen of Socinus.

From Luslawice an active correspondence was maintained with the churches of Poland and Transylvania, and it might be truly said of Socinus that he could "see of the travail of his soul and be satisfied" at the growth of the Socinian congregations in strength and unity everywhere. Rakow, under the friendly patronage of John Sieninski, waiwode of Podolia, who had turned Socinian in 1600, became a hotbed of Socinian propaganda. A famous printing press issued the works of Socinus and other scholars,[10] and in 1602 a school which was virtually a university was established, and enjoyed a tremendous popularity.

It was a source of great satisfaction to Socinus that his dear friend, Peter Stoinski, who resided in the neighborhood, was a frequent visitor. Although he was far from well, and was indeed prepared for death at any time, Socinus does not seem to have anticipated the fatal issue of his illness. A letter to his old friend Schmalz, dated January 23, 1604,[11] makes no mention of his own health, but contains the usual friendly counsel about dealing with a difficult local situation and expresses the writer's pleasant anticipation of at-

FAUSTUS SOCINUS

tending the coming synod at Rakow which was not far away.

When his last call came on March 3rd, Socinus was ready. Though his church was strong and united, he was weary with the strife and controversy, and eager to go to his reward, as he declared to the faithful Stoinski, who was at his side. Socinus' belief in immortality had always been a strong one, and as he drew his last breath he declared to Stoinski his joy in being released from his labors and obtaining his reward.

Stoinski, "the companion of his life and labors," preached the funeral oration, and in the following year, when scarcely forty years of age, joined his comrade.

NOTES

1. In his letter to Wadowitz (*Opera* I, 475) he specifically disclaims such a title.

2. a. Socinus always considered his *Against the Atheists* his ablest work; unforunately the only manuscript was destroyed in the Krakow riot of 1598.
 b. A brief tract against the weird conception of the origin of Christ's body held by the Mennonites (*Opera* II, 461-463).
 c. He wrote a brief tract *Against the Chiliasts* (*Opera* II, 457-461) 1589, and some "notes" found in the same volume 446-448.
 d. Not to mention the lengthy controversy with David, a celebrated disputation held with Christian Franken in 1584. (*Opera* II, 767ff.)

3. This letter is dated March, 1583, see *Opera* I, 508-510.

4. In the letter quoted above, Socinus refers to his dispute with the Posen Jesuits and the activity of the order in Krakow; "there are already more than enough Jesuits in Krakow, and so far as I hear, they will establish a fixed residence here." (*Opera* I, 509^b).

5. The foregoing account of the riot is taken in most part from the vivid description found in Fock (Op. cit. 177ff.).

6. See the letter to Wadowitz (*Opera* I, 477^b).

CONFLICT AND CONSUMMATION

7. There is an excellent English translation with a concise and accurate introduction, by Thomas Rees, London, 1818.

8. *Quod Regni Poloniae & Magni Ducatus Lithuaniae homines, vulgo Evangelici dicti, qui solidae pietatis sunt studiosi, omnino deberent se illorum coetui adjungere, qui in iisdem locis falso atque immerito Arriani atque Ebionitae vocantur."* (July 1599) (*Opera* I, 691 ff.)

9. This school, which the Socinians proudly termed the *Athenae Sarmaticae*, was attended by other Protestants and Catholics as well as Unitarians, as proselyting was not practised. The renowned faculty and careful curriculum attracted over one thousand students a year for a considerable period. Its glory was cut short by the action of the Diet in 1638 which closed the school, banished the professors, confiscated the press, and dispersed the congregation, using as a pretext the wanton prank of some students.

10. Alexander Rodecki was first in charge of the press and was succeeded by Sebastian Sternacki who married his only daughter. See Sand, Op. cit. p. 201.

11. *Opera* I, 468.

CHAPTER X

A GENTLEMAN AND A SCHOLAR

AN IDEA of Socinus' appearance can be gained from the engraving prefixed to his *Opera*, Vol. I, and to the brief biography by Przypkowski (1636) and from the graphic description of that writer. We are told that Socinus was of middle height and somewhat inclined to be stout. A high forehead and fine eyes were his most conspicuous features, while his expression suggested a happy combination of courtly kindness and masculine force. He was simple in his habits and unostentatious in his dress.

There is probably not a single outstanding figure of the Reformation or its aftermath whose opinions have been more bitterly assailed, but whose character and attainments have been less subject to attack, than Faustus Socinus.

Were we to rely upon that early biography of Przypkowski we might be accused of uncritically accepting the adulation of a devoted follower and kinsman. If the glowing panegyric of Toulmin were our only more recent authority, we might be blamed for hearkening to the paean of the "Enlightenment" which found such a notable fore-

A GENTLEMAN AND A SCHOLAR

runner in Socinus. So, disregarding the natural admiration of such writers as Przypkowski, Biddle, Bayle, and Toulmin, let us consider the verdict of Socinus' most bitter opponents, Roman Catholics and orthodox Protestants.

Père Guichard, author of the *Histoire du Socinianisme*[1] is louder in his praise of the virtues and gifts of Socinus than he is in the denunciation of his doctrines. This writer admits the substantial accuracy of Przypkowski's glowing praise, and sums up Socinus' conduct in a simple but effective sentence—"his morals were without reproach." Socinus, he admits, had "an ardent love for that which he believed to be the truth, a generous compassion for the poor, a piety for God which can be by no means denied, an indefatigable zeal for the churches, a patience in the testing of everything, a greatness of soul which raised him above persecutions, or which avoided them by a great virtue."[2]

One of the most pleasing features of the career of Socinus is his unfailing courtesy and good temper. In an age that was marked by the most acrimonious theological disputes in which even men like Calvin and Luther stooped to the language of the street when inveighing against their opponents, Socinus remained a gentleman and a Christian. His controversial works like the *Concerning the Saver* and the disputations with

FAUSTUS SOCINUS

Niemojewski on Baptism are all the more cogent because of their spirit of fair play and good-will.

The learned German historian Mosheim, who deplored the revival of Socinianism in the *Aufklärung*, and who chided the English for unofficially tolerating the harried sect, has no criticism to make of the character of Socinus. Commenting upon the change wrought in the state of the Unitarian churches in Poland following the advent of Socinus, he declares: "The affairs of the Unitarians assumed a new aspect under the dexterity and industry of Faustus Socinus, a man of superior genius, of moderate learning, of a firm and resolute spirit, less erudite than his uncle, Laelius, but more bold and courageous." [3]

Socinus' literary and theological attainments have been often "damned with faint praise" or compared slightingly with those of his uncle, Laelius. It is not our purpose here to evaluate the relative attainments of the two men, but if Laelius was a ripe scholar, the same may be said of his nephew. A schoolman, Faustus certainly was not, nor did he desire such a reputation; a scholar of no mean ability he undoubtedly was.

The humanism of his native Tuscany was deeply ingrained in the thought of Socinus. The delightful prose of Boccacio and Poggio Bracciolini appealed to him, but it was poetry that commanded his own literary interests and powers.

A GENTLEMAN AND A SCHOLAR

One meets occasional reminiscences of Virgil and other classic poets in his works, and there is at least one long quotation from Dante. In his earlier years, Socinus had tried his own hand at poetry and had produced some fairly creditable although rather doleful sonnets.[4] A certain young lady named Delia had also inspired this Muse, and we have already alluded to his Italian poetical version of the Psalms begun at Basel, but apparently never completed.

The great bulk of Socinus' theological works were composed in Latin—a Latin that is fluent rather than elegant, and is sometimes labored and involved. Some of the earlier works such as the *Concerning the Authority of Holy Scripture* and the *Commentary on the First Chapter of John's Gospel* were first composed in Italian and later translated.

Socinus' mastery of Greek is apparent in his exegetical works. His acquaintance with Hebrew is less strongly marked, the few references to the original being stock quotations or familiar words; but his knowledge of modern languages has been often overlooked. That he knew German may be inferred from his sojourns in Basel and Zürich, and from the considerable number of German theologians such as Francken and Schomann with whom he was in constant contact in Poland. Evidently Socinus' employment in Lyons had given him a good working knowledge of French, for his correspondence with the Fleming Spangenberg was conducted in that language.[5] Although he was not a young man upon his arrival in Poland, Socinus mastered its difficult language, and his controversy with Niemojewski, in which he repeatedly refers to the Polish rendering of Scripture, shows his familiarity with that tongue.

The skill of Socinus as a student of the Bible is universally admitted, and his *Concerning the Authority of Holy Scripture* remained a standard work on the subject for two hundred years. His honesty in recognizing the differences within the Bible, especially between the moral teaching of the Old Testament and that of the New, and the divergent treatment of immortality in each, marks him as a forerunner of the modern critical student of the Scriptures.

Frequent examples of Socinus' skill as a textual critic might be adduced, but a typical instance must suffice. In the defence of the orthodox doctrine of the nature of the Holy Spirit, Socinus' Jesuit opponents had adduced texts from I Corinthians. Socinus answers: "Greek codices, with which the Syriac Version agrees, do not have *Et portate*, I Cor. 6:20," and he rules out this gloss which is found in the Vulgate, in certain old Latin texts, and in several Fathers, but which does not occur in any important uncial MSS.[6] Modern text-

A GENTLEMAN AND A SCHOLAR

ual scholarship universally confirms Socinus' judgment.

In his exegesis, which was greatly respected in his own day, Socinus resembles Calvin in his insistence upon the *literal* meaning; unlike Calvin he does not go further to indulge in the vagaries of allegory, while he admits the use of metaphor on certain occasions. According to Socinus *recta* or *sana ratio* is to be the student's guide in the exegesis of the Bible.

A typical example of the soundness of Socinus' exegesis is his exposition of the Lord's Prayer in his commentary on the Sermon on the Mount.[7] Socinus gives here due credit to other scholars, such as Erasmus and Ruarus, compares variant readings, detects latent Hebraisms, and evaluates the relative strength of the Matthean and Lucan versions, etc. His conclusions are always well argued and never far-fetched, nor do they betray evidences of prejudice.

To Socinus' work in the field of theology, where his most important contributions lie, we now turn for a more extended treatment.

NOTES

1. Przypkowski's brief biography (first published separately in 1636) contains this engraving. Unfortunately most of the extant copies of the *Opera* lack this interesting frontispiece. The only modern work reproducing this sole portrait of Socinus is Van Slee's *De Geschiednis van het Socinianisme in der Nederlanden, Haarlem;* 1914.
2. Opus cit. p. 384-385.

FAUSTUS SOCINUS

3. *History, Century XVI*, Sec. II, pt. 2, Par. 11.
4. Gordon (*Encyclopaedia Britannica*, note on Article) mentions specimens to be found in Ferentilli's *Scelta di Stanze di Diversi Authori Toscanini* (1579, 1594), also others given in Cantu's *Gli Eretici d'Italia*, (1866), II., and the *Athenaeum* 11th August, 1877 (Brady's researches).
5. *Opera* I. 478ff.
6. *Opera* II. 429^b (*Assert. 14^1*)
7. *Opera* I. 40^{b}ff (*Explicatio Capitis Sexti*, Vers. 9ff.)

PART TWO

THE TEACHING OF FAUSTUS SOCINUS

CHAPTER XI

THE NORM OF DOCTRINE

SOCINIANISM had this in common with the other Reformation faiths, that it professed to be a return to the faith and practice of the New Testament; but whereas the Lutherans and Calvinists made a notable contribution in recovering something of the simplicity, democracy, and enthuiasm of the primitive church, they reproduced essentially the same body of doctrine that had been held since Augustine. In fact, it might almost be said that Luther and Calvin represented in their theologies a conservative tendency in opposing the rational theologies of the medieval renaissance by the more austere systems of Augustine and Anselm. To put it briefly, a radical change in the religious life, but not in the religious thought of Europe was effected by the Reformers. It was Socinus and the other Antitrinitarians of the sixteenth and seventeenth centuries who attempted a really thoroughgoing reconstruction of Christian ideas upon the basis of a rational approach to the New Testament.

The Socinian search for religious truth went along the two paths of scriptural exegesis and rational inquiry.[1] Socinus, himself, was much more "biblical" in his language and emphasis than were many of his successors. It cannot be denied that he conscientiously believed that he derived the whole of his doctrinal system from Scripture. In this respect Socinus is in the succession of that whole group of Anabaptist-Antitrinitarian thinkers that originated for the most part in North Italy.[2] Fock neatly summarizes the primary importance assigned by his school to Scripture: "The Holy Scriptures have importance in the Socinian system; the religious revelations which were imparted to individual godly men are thus mediated to the generality. Christ has received the Gospel of the Truth from the mouth of God, from him the Apostles and first Christians obtained it, and they have set it down for posterity in the Holy Scriptures."[3] When, for example, he teaches that the doctrine of the Trinity must be abandoned because it is nowhere clearly taught in the New Testament, one cannot contest the soundness of his scriptural position. It is, however, more than likely that Socinus' original objection to the dogma sprang from rational rather than from scriptural soil. This is the more apparent in his fundamental rejection of the doctrine of satisfaction. That Christ died in man's stead to satisfy the divine justice or to appease the divine wrath is rejected by Socinus on both scrip-

THE NORM OF DOCTRINE

tural and rational grounds, but it is noteworthy that the arguments from the rational side are much the stronger.[4]

Dr. Karl Müller in his monumental *Kirchengeschichte* emphasizes this appeal to reason as *der starke rationale Zug* of Socinianism; he couples with this rationalistic tendency a strong humanist strain derived from the early Antitrinitarian background of Socinus' teaching: "So we have before us a new and peculiar structure of religion and the church. Its roots lie all intertwined in the soil of the romantic humanists from Servetus to Chateillon and Aconzio, and above all the Baptist Council of Venice in 1550 shows to a most extraordinary degree the fundamentals of his theology."[5]

Later writers, such as Ruarus and Krell, did not hesitate to use *recta ratio* (right reason) or *sana ratio* (sound reason) as the criterion for dogma, but Socinus was always careful to insist upon giving first place to *auctoritas Sanctae Scripturae* (authority of Holy Scripture), and adduced rational arguments rather as corroborative evidence.

To believe that Socinus was a bibliolater of the modern "plenary inspiration" type, is wholly to mistake his use of scripture. The Old Testament, according to Socinus, was far inferior to the New, and he adduces with evident relish comparisons between the precepts of Jesus and the Mosaic Law, showing the superiority of the former in each case.[6] Nor is it correct to say that it is the teaching of the whole New Testament as opposed to the Old Testament that is considered normative by Socinus. He recognizes very definitely that there is a Bible within the Bible, namely, the teaching of Jesus. In this respect Socinus showed his originality and sound sense, for whereas Luther and Calvin accepted an Augustinian dogmatic that went back directly to Paul rather than to Jesus, Socinus took his stand definitely upon the teaching of Jesus. Even this modicum of normative Scripture is for practical purposes further reduced and the Teaching of Jesus is usually equivalent to the Sermon on the Mount. Harnack observes on this point: "The foremost position is now assigned to the New Testament in the doctrine of religion. All fanatical elements are suppressed. That the New Testament is the sole regulative authority, source, and norm of religion cannot be declared more positively and dryly than by Socinianism. *The Christian religion is the Theology of the New Testament*."[7] As we have suggested, we would restrict Harnack's definition still more closely and maintain that the Christian religion for Socinus is the Theology of the Gospels (as opposed to the Pauline Theology), or even the Theology of Jesus.

THE NORM OF DOCTRINE

One cannot but admire the fidelity with which Socinus and his followers related their dogmatic and ethical systems to the teaching of Jesus. Again and again we find Socinus appealing to the *praecepta Christi* as the final authority on some moot point of theology or morals. In the ethical sphere, this fidelity to the Sermon on the Mount cost the Socinians dear, for whereas conventional Protestant morality, with its emphasis upon the private (and often the Old Testament) virtues, was admirably suited to the whole fabric of a commercial, middle-class society and to the growing spirit of nationalism, the religious tolerance, absolute pacifism, uncompromising opposition to capital punishment, and the refusal of political preferments on the part of the Socinians, were considered detrimental to patriotism and seem to have contributed as much as the actual Jesuit opposition to the downfall of the Socinian church in Poland.[8]

It can be argued with justice that the Socinians, in insisting upon the letter rather than upon the spirit of Jesus' teaching, missed the forest for the trees, and laid themselves open to numerous anachronisms. In attempting to escape the old legalism, they were in danger of creating an infinitely superior, but no less authoritarian system. On the other hand it cannot be denied that the return of Socinus to the actual teaching of Jesus as the

[89]

norm of Christian faith and practice anticipated by three centuries the whole "Back to Jesus" movement of our own time. It can be said to the advantage of the Socinians, however, that they appear to have taken this position with much more earnestness and sincerity than most of our modern churches have shown, for they refused to compromise with the growing burgher and chauvinistic standards of their day and went down with colors flying. Our modern churches have too often acquiesced in the *status quo;* witness their impotence in the face of the World War, and their belated efforts on behalf of social justice. Our modern churches might well emulate the spirit of sacrificial devotion to the teaching of Christ that was found in these earnest "modernists" of another day. Perhaps, if another war impends, they may, like the Socinians, say, "Christians may not participate in war," [9] and perhaps they will condemn some of the sins of our present social order as out of line with "the precepts of Christ."

NOTES

1. There is a rather interesting division of opinion among scholars as to the relative importance of reason and Scripture in Socinus' theology. Mosheim (op. cit., 709-710), followed by a large number of more recent scholars, has assigned a primary position to reason. Harnack (*History of Dogma,* vol. VII, p. 138ff.) and others emphasize the Biblical basis to which Socinus appealed. On the whole I feel rather inclined to agree with Harnack, although I feel that I can sense a kind of unconscious undercurrent of rationalism in many of Socinus' most scriptural arguments.

THE NORM OF DOCTRINE

For an interesting nineteenth century controversy on the subject, see Ziegler's article in Henke's *Neue Magazin für Religions Philosophie* etc., Vol. IV, pt. 2, p. 204 (for the Biblical basis), and Schrökh in his *Kirchengeschichte seit die Reformation,* Vol. V, p. 560 (for the rational basis).

2. The best account of this group still appears to be Trechsel's *Die Antitrinitarier vor Faustus Socinus,* Heidelberg, 1844.

3. Op. cit., 325.

4. See his argument in the *Praelectiones Theologicae,* Ch. 15 ff., *Opera* I, 564 ff., and the criticisms in Fock, op. cit., 615ff., Harnack, op. cit., 156 ff, Ritschl, *Justification and Reconciliation* (1st German ed.), 316 ff., Shedd, *History of Christian Doctrine,* Bk. V, ch. 7, pt. 2.

5. IV-2-2, 133.

6. Guichard, op. cit, 389, cites this as one of Socinus' errors "sur la foi," namely "That the moral precepts of the New Testament are different from the moral precepts of the Old." Cf. Fock, op. cit., 325ff.

7. Op. cit., vol. VII, 138.

8. See Part II, Ch. 8, of the present work.

9. See *Opera* I, 463*.

CHAPTER XII

GOD, ONE IN ESSENCE AND LORD OF ALL

AT no point has the Socinian theology been more strenuously assailed than in its fundamental conception of God; not only has Socinus' arch-heresy, the denial of the Trinity, been combated by orthodox writers from Wujek down to the present time, but in recent years there has been a tendency to attack Socinus' doctrine of the Divine Sovereignty as a pale reproduction of the medieval Scotist position.

Socinus was so deeply impressed with the unity of God that he was led to deny the dogma of the Trinity, thus incurring the wrath of orthodoxy. He laid equal stress upon the Sovereignty (*imperium*) of the One God, and in so doing was led to so exclusive an emphasis on the divine will as to bring on himself in our day the charge of plagiarising Duns Scotus, the great fourteenth century schoolman.

The dogma of the Trinity is repudiated by Socinus as unscriptural, unreasonable, and unnecessary. Conceding that the language of Scripture may sometimes be construed as attributing deity

GOD, ONE IN ESSENCE

to other than "the one God, who is Jehovah," Socinus maintains that this is a figure of speech. In his brief summary, *An Examination of the Argument for the Three and One God*,[1] he declares: "the name of Deity is received in Scripture principally in a double sense. The first way is when it is said that God is one. The other sense is when it signifies one who has some supreme control, power, or dominion from the one God Himself, or for some other reason is partaker of the divinity of this one God. Hence, for example, the one God, namely Jehovah, is called God of Gods (Ps. 50:1). In this other sense, the Son or Christ, is occasionally called God in Holy Scripture."

In short, Socinus makes the distinction between Deity and Divinity drawn by some modern theologians who would deny that Christ has a place in the God-head, but who strenuously maintain his divine relationship to the Father. This point is driven further by Socinus in subsequent paragraphs: "For this distinction, one essence and three persons, nowhere occurs in Holy Scripture, and is manifestly opposed to most certain reason and truth."[2] And again: "For even if Christ is occasionally called God, as was said above, nevertheless the name of God does not then signify actual substance, but simply an attribute of substance."

FAUSTUS SOCINUS

Socinus, therefore, did not deny the charge that he repudiated the dogma of the Trinity, but attempted, rather, to give scriptural and rational arguments for his Unitarian position. As we shall see in the following chapter he did not relegate the Person of Christ to the position of a merely human figure, as did many of the eighteenth century Deists and modern Unitarians, but assigned to Jesus a kind of intermediate position, wholly human but especially endowed with divine wisdom, power, and virtue.

The second objection, that Socinus was a pure voluntarist in his doctrine of God and simply reproduced the teaching of Scotus, has been urged with great force by the late Professor Lindsay of Glasgow.[3] That there is a parallel cannot be denied, but to accuse Socinus of simply taking over the Scotist doctrine and republishing it is an unwarranted overstatement.

In the first place it may be said that Socinus knew very little of Duns Scotus, or for that matter of any of the medieval philosophers at first hand. He admits, in one of his last letters (December 15, 1603 N. S.), that "he had never studied philosophy or come in contact with (what they call) scholastic theology."[4] The whole Thomist-Scotist controversy on the *perseitas boni* (the goodness inherent in God's nature) would have seemed meaningless to the naïve and

[94]

GOD, ONE IN ESSENCE

practical mind of Socinus, whose emphasis on the Divine Will was practical rather than metaphysical. It is possible, however, that the general tone of Franciscan preaching in North Italy, which was strongly tinctured with Scotism, may have had an unconscious effect upon Socinus. It is indubitable that Socinus stressed an unquestioning and complete obedience to the revealed will of God and that he laid an emphasis upon the Divine Sovereignty that is scarcely less marked than in Calvin's writings. It should be noted, however, that Socinus excludes predestination absolutely; in this respect he differs again from the "straddling position" of Scotus.

Socinus' emphasis upon the will of God has a most practical and ethical turn. In his Second Epistle to Radecki,[5] he says: "Now assuredly the foundation of our salvation is God and Christ, but not in so far as we correctly know their essence and substance, but in so far as we keep the will of God declared through Christ."

While Socinus approaches the Scotist position that what is good depends upon the good pleasure of God (i. e. because God arbitrarily willed it to be good), he never states the position as baldly as does the schoolman. Like Scotus, Socinus strenuously avoided an anthropomorphic view of Deity, but he did allow certain very definite attributes of God to be postulated, as we shall see in a moment.

The real weakness of Socinus' view of God does not consist, in my opinion, in his anti-trinitarian or allegedly voluntarist views. I would consider these, on the contrary, to be elements of the original insight and strength in his system. The inadequacy of his formally expressed doctrine of God is due rather to the essentially external and juridical nature of his whole system. In his uncompleted *Institute of the Christian Religion*,[6] Socinus reiterates his fundamental position on the unity of God and the duty of obedience to His will. He strongly emphasizes the sole supreme and eternal sovereignty (*imperium*) of God, and then answers the question: "Are there not other things, besides, pertaining to the nature of God?" As the Master in the dialogue he replies that there are three: Justice (Righteousness and Equity), Wisdom (The science and knowledge of things), and Power (The means of doing what He wills). This trinity of characteristics is elaborated with skill and clarity, but we cannot help feeling that the Deity described is transcendent and austere to the point of coldness. When we come to the end of the section we sympathize with the Pupil when he asks: "Does not the goodness of God pertain to His very essence? Is it not necessary for us to know that God is good?" But

GOD, ONE IN ESSENCE

the Master coldly squelches this childish query: "In so far as the goodness of God pertains to His essence, it is also included wholly in righteousness and equity, which under the head of Justice has already been mentioned." It is enough to "keep the precepts of God given us through Christ," and it is idle to seek any "natural goodness" outside the voluntary goodness of God, concludes the Master.[7]

It is only fair to say that in his private correspondence Socinus speaks of God in more personal language and with greater warmth, but the fact remains that God is for him, as for Grotius, a great Sovereign and Law-giver who is to be obeyed rather than loved. If the fiery zeal and generous affection of Luther could have been added to the sane and noble character of Socinus, perhaps in Socinianism, the immanence of God would have supplemented His transcendence, and the Divine Justice would have been tempered with the Divine Love.

NOTES

1. *Opera* I, 281-282.
2. *Opera* I, 282^a.
3. *History of the Reformation*, Book V, ch. 3,—Lindsay may have derived his position from hints in Ritschl's *Justification and Reconciliation*, Eng. Trans., 1900, 265 ff. & Harnack op. cit. 144 ff.
4. *Opera* I, 490^a.
5. *Opera* I, 374^a.
6. *Opera* I, 651-652.
7. *Opera* I, 653.

CHAPTER XIII

JESUS CHRIST, THE SON OF GOD

SOCINUS' doctrine of Christ has provoked an opposition that is all the more vehement because of its basic misconceptions. To the ordinary supporter of orthodoxy, Socinus' denial of the Trinity meant the relegation of Jesus to a purely human rôle, and even his better-informed opponents have overlooked, for the most part, Socinus' principal work on the Person of Christ, the *Concerning the Nature or Essence of Jesus Christ, the Son of God*, and have confined their observations to the famous *Concerning the Saver*, which deals with the work rather than the person of Christ.

In his written disputation with the Reformed scholar, Andrew Wolan (Volanus), Socinus systematically propounded his doctrine of the person of Christ.[1] In this carefully prepared treatise, Socinus began with a general refutation of a work by Wolan that had been published as an attack on the Unitarians, and then for the benefit of those who had not seen Wolan's work, proceeded to attack the latter's arguments *seriatim*.

Wolan had resented the attack made by *Anon-*

JESUS CHRIST, THE SON OF GOD

ymus (Socinus) upon himself and others "who confess Christ to be partaker of the Divine Nature from eternity," and sharer in all the Divine glory and prerogatives. The gist of Socinus' answer is that the exalted position of Jesus is one that has been conferred upon Him as a special favor (*beneficium*) by God, and that the unique power of Jesus is a result of His perfect obedience to the Divine will.

To Wolan's claim: "All the glory whatsoever is due the Father, the Son claims for Himself, and he who does not honor the Son, does not honor the Father, and he who has not the Son, has not the Father," Socinus simply answers: "It is true, undoubtedly true, that he who does not honor the Son, neither honors the Father, and that he who does not have the Son does not have the Father, as the divine oracles plainly testify. However, it does not follow that all glory whatsoever that is due the Father, is due the Son"—this, declares Socinus, is a logical fallacy.[2]

Wolan touches the very heart of the whole problem when he claims that Jesus is termed God in the Scriptures, and that the Divine power (*virtus*) in him is attested by his various works and miracles which He was able to accomplish only as God. Wolan also maintained the position of Christ as the Divine Logos or agent in the cosmic creation. Socinus answers that the Deity of

FAUSTUS SOCINUS

Christ is not to be inferred from his miracles or his power, as these were found also in the prophets and apostles; he feels, moreover, that the word *Deus* is being overworked by his opponent. On the second point, Socinus maintains that the one God (*Jehovah*) is the sole author of good and the sole creator of the universe.

To the charge that his party did not worship or pray to Christ, Socinus enters a flat denial and adduces his controversy with Francis David. Christ may be approached as our helper, he declares, and quotes with approval that section of the epistle to the Hebrews relating to Christ's function as the exalted high priest.

The lengthy section of the *Concerning the Nature* that deals with Christ's saving work we may pass by here as belonging properly to the next chapter, realizing that the whole subject is fully covered in a special work, the *Concerning the Saver.*

Wolan's claim that both Genesis and the Pauline epistles attest that Christ is the agent of creation, is met by the ingenious explanation that the creation described in Genesis I is not the same as that referred to in Colossians I. The subject matter of Moses is the visible creation; that of Paul is admittedly "the mystery of the exhibiting and manifesting of Christ." This second creation, declares Socinus, quoting his previous response, is

JESUS CHRIST, THE SON OF GOD

the reformation that Christ worked in human nature.[3]

Wolan's charge that *Anonymus* had avoided the issue of the pre-existence of Christ and the testimony of Scripture that He came forth from God is answered in an ingenious but rather fantastic way by Socinus. In the first place, the prophets are adduced as God-sent messengers; but when pinned down to certain Johannine texts Socinus is compelled to postulate a special sojourn of Christ in heaven taking place at some point between his birth and crucifixion.[4]

After a discussion on scriptural interpretation, Socinus makes a somewhat feeble reply to the key text, John 8:58, "Before Abraham was, I am." Wolan's argument from Romans 9:5: "Who is over all, God blessed for ever," is more adequately met, and the clause is referred to the Father on the authority of Erasmus, for whose judgment Socinus had the highest regard.

The stock charge that he and his colleagues are Ebionites is resented by Socinus, who declares, "There is no objection to the adoration of Christ," but this is not to be put upon the same plane as the adoration of God. Other passages are considered, and in each case Socinus maintains the supreme position of God as the object of worship (*cultus*) and assigns a subordinate position to the worship of Christ.

FAUSTUS SOCINUS

Wolan has repeated the time-honored argument of all orthodox theologians that his opponents are arrogantly assuming a position superior to that of the ancient fathers or the recent reformers. Socinus frankly answers that men are continually receiving new light through the kindness of God and reminds Wolan that he, in common with Protestants in general, had repudiated certain opinions common in the early church, such as the invocation of the saints. Socinus concludes this section by asking Wolan: "Do not numberless men as well as churches today feel just the same as I do, and not merely in one part, but in many parts of the Christian world?"

The remainder of Socinus' work is taken up largely with answering another time-honored charge that he was simply repeating old heresies; the Ebionites, Cerinthus, Paul of Samosata, the Sabellians, the Arians, the Nestorians, and the Eutychians had been adduced in proof by Wolan. It is significant that of these only Paul of Samosata (and Photinus) is recognized by Socinus as a kindred spirit, and the Italian remarks that the works of the Antiochene bishop are no longer extant.[5]

We can appreciate how radical was the Christological position of Socinus by comparing some of its main features with those of Calvin, who on this point was typically orthodox. In his import-

JESUS CHRIST, THE SON OF GOD

ant work the *Concerning Offences*,[6] Calvin, under the heading, *Offences Derived from Doctrine*, mentions the dogmas of the two natures of Christ, salvation through Christ's satisfaction made on the Cross, our blessing resulting from Christ becoming a curse for us, total human depravity, and others. We find that all these doctrines, considered essential by the orthodox, are completely repudiated by Socinus.

The foregoing account of Socinus' view of Christ is drawn from his primary work on the subject, the *Concerning the Nature*, but it must be remembered that this work is controversial in nature and consists in defence and attack rather than in reasoned statement. In his *Institute of the Christian Religion*,[7] Socinus declares his positive convictions. Christ is human (*homo*), born of a virgin *sine viri ope*, conceived and formed in the strength of the divine spirit, "a true man like us in all things, excepting sin," "subject to suffering and death" (*patibilis et mortalis*) during his earthly career, but after his exaltation not subject to suffering and death. Christ's unique divine sonship (*divina filiatio*) is guaranteed for Socinus by the virgin birth; that there is any metaphysical relation in nature or essence between Christ and God is, however, expressly denied. The two names of the Lord, Jesus, the proper name, signifying that he was to be the savior of the people, and the royal name, Christ, declaring his kingly authority over the people, are both bestowed on him by God.

The Christology of Socinus is unique and was the most rational approach to the subject yet made; the fanciful features of the Arian, Sabellian, and Servetian systems are wholly lacking, and the retention of such a dogma as the virgin birth or the propounding of such a theory as the heavenly sojourn, are attempts to do justice to the letter of Scripture. The unique character of Socinus' Christology is not derived from its negations (the denial of the Deity of Christ and of His eternity from all time), for these were the common property of all the Antitrinitarians, but consists in both the rational and the moral values of his position; to him as to Pascal "Jesus Christ stands alone in his own order of holiness," and the Italian reformer attempted to discard what appeared to him to be unnecessary and unreasonable accretions, and to present Jesus as divinely human. A real and valuable emphasis is placed upon the voluntary obedience of Jesus to God's will, and the necessity for us to follow his example and teaching as the "interpreter of God." Nor are the more mystical relations between the believer and Christ precluded by Socinus. He firmly maintains the continuing existence and accessibility of Jesus, who may be approached directly

JESUS CHRIST, THE SON OF GOD

in prayer and adoration, and who is the mighty vicegerent of God.[8]

NOTES

1. This work appeared anonymously in Latin in the autumn of 1583, but was later openly dedicated by the author to the Polish magnate and patron of the Socinians, John Kiszka. (June 14, 1588). See *Opera* II, 370 ff.
2. *Opera* II, 384ᵇ.
3. *Opera* II, 398-399.
4. "And as in a previous reply I not obscurely affirmed, so do I now hereby affirm, and so far insist, that Christ after he was born of Mary, and before he arose from the dead, was really and actually in heaven; that very man, Jesus of Nazareth, in that intervening period, was at some time in heaven, I by all means insist." *Opera* II, 403ᵇ. This point is further developed in the *Institution of the Christian Religion*, (*Opera* I, 675) where Socinus declares that Jesus before commencing his God-given work was in the very presence of God, where he received express instruction regarding his mission—and more especially his teaching. Socinus compares this sojourn with Moses' stay upon Mount Sinai. The theory proves valuable as supporting Socinus' insistence upon complete and unquestioning obedience to the words of Christ; it is also an illustration of the far-fetched theories that occasionally appear in Socinus' clearly reasoned theology—theories that are necessitated by an unquestioning acceptance of the "ipsissima verba" of Christ. Guichard gives an excellent and accurate summary of this position. (Opus cit. p. 388).
5. See especially p. 421ᵇ. Only a very few fragments of the writing of Paul of Samosata were known in the sixteenth century, but in recent years several important fragments have been discovered. While there are several striking parallels between Socinus and Paul, the former could not have found his theology in the few fragments of the Antiochene bishop then extant. Paul, moreover, had a kind of doctrine of the Logos which was wholly alien to the thought of Socinus.
6. The *De Scandalis* published in Latin and French at Geneva in 1551.
7. *Opera* I, 653 ff. This work, which is incomplete, extends through the Doctrine of Christ.
8. Jesus, for Socinus, is not merely a historical personage, as held by modern left-wing Unitarians; he occupies a unique and exalted position at the right hand of God, and has been invested by the Father with all power and authority. See *Opera* I, 655-656, and *passim*. Fock, op. cit. 536 ff. has an excellent paragraph upon this point.

CHAPTER XIV

FREE OBEDIENCE, THE WAY OF LIFE

"FUNDAMENTAL in the teaching of the Socinians was the moral ability of man," declares McGiffert in his illuminating treatment of the school of Socinus.[1] Equally important was Socinus' insistence upon the necessity of man's obedience to the precepts of Christ as the means of attaining salvation (or eternal life).[2]

Socinus' rejection of the doctrines of particular predestination and election, original sin and total depravity, redemption by the propitiation of Christ on the Cross and justification by an act of faith on the part of the believer, shows not only his basic cleavage with the theology of the Roman Church which he had left, but an even more basic cleavage with the Reformed and Lutheran Churches with which he attempted to live on friendly terms. Socinus' antipathy to these dogmas, all of which were held with particular tenacity by the Calvinists, appears to be a product of a double influence native to his Sienese heritage. There was the strongly humanistic influence derived from the Piccolominis on his moth-

FREE OBEDIENCE

er's side and from his father's brilliant brothers, an influence which tended to emphasize the capacity of the individual; and there was, secondly, the clear, logical, legal strain coming from his father, grandfather, and all the long line of jurists that had made the name Sozzini famous—an influence that led him to reject dogmas that appeared to him absurd, unjust, and impractical.

The Augustinian doctrine of predestination, involving the election of certain individuals to eternal felicity and the foreordination of others to "dishonor and wrath," with the accompanying concept of the Divine foreknowledge of particular events, was completely rejected by Socinus. In his interesting *Theological Lectures* (*Praelectiones Theologicae*), Socinus selects the key texts for both sides of the controversy and thus states his view: "This famous passage in the same Paul (Phil. 2:13) must be evaluated: 'For it is God which worketh in you both to will and to do of His good pleasure.' Now surely if it is God who effects in us our willing and not merely our doing, nothing, not even what concerns the will, will be in our power. I reply, that as it has been stated by me above, it is not to be doubted that God should be termed the very author of our good will, but I, nevertheless, deny that it follows on that account that we accomplish nothing freely in that respect, seeing that just before these words are recited, it stands written: 'Work out your own salvation with fear and trembling.' " And Socinus goes on to point out that some of the unpleasant features in the life of the Philippian community could scarcely be attributed to the volition or the operation of God.[3]

In the fifth chapter of the *Lectures*, Socinus urges with great force that if the first man before the fall had been endowed with free will there was no reason why man should have been deprived of free will after the fall, "since neither the nature of the case demands it nor the justice of God permits it."[4]

Like Pelagius, Socinus denies the existence of original sin. In the fourth chapter of the *Lectures*,[5] he declares that whether sin be conceived of as guilt (*culpa*) or penalty (*poena*) it is rooted in the will of the individual. Original sin is impossible since the newborn babe has no conscious will. The key text of the proponents of the doctrine of original sin, Psalm 51:7, "Behold I was shapen in iniquity and in sin did my mother conceive me," is explained as "a figure of speech and a hyperbole," and other passages are compared with similar interpretations.

"Let us conclude, therefore, that even improperly speaking there is no original sin, that is, from the sin of the first parent, no taint or depravity inborn of necessity in all human kind, nor

FREE OBEDIENCE

in any way inflicted." In these words Socinus sweepingly rejects the Calvinistic theories of total depravity and original sin, even as he rejects that of Calvinistic predestination.

The denial of the doctrines of total depravity and original sin is supplemented by Socinus' repudiation of the orthodox doctrine of the divine justice. We have noted in a previous chapter that Socinus considers justice one of the three divine characteristics (*res ad Dei naturam pertinentes*). In the *Institution*[6] he declares: "We ought, therefore, to be persuaded that God is supremely and most perfectly just, that He is righteous (*rectus*) and fair (*aequus*). And he goes on to say that in obedience to the divine will man is to avail himself, though unworthy, of God's blessings, and that any evil encountered is not to be traced to the authorship of God.

That justice in God is more than a quality or characteristic, Socinus will not admit. He utterly denies the contemporary view of the divine justice as fixed, immutable, and necessary in the nature of God, and demanding when offended a corresponding and complete satisfaction. Let us then examine at some length Socinus' conception of the divine justice as simply righteousness (*rectitudo*) and fairness (*aequitas*),[7] for this conception is basic for his complete rejection of the doctrine of satisfaction, and is the groundwork for his chief work, the *Concerning Jesus Christ, the Saver*. In this famous work he writes: "But you will say that it is necessary for God's justice to be satisfied—that kind of justice which you contend must be wholly satisfied does not reside in God, but is an effect of His will. For when God punishes sinners, since we call this work of His by some worthy name, we say that He then employs justice; likewise when He spares some offender, the Scripture says that He has employed mercy. Wherefore, it is not necessary for God to have that kind of justice satisfied, or to revoke it.—For God never does nor can do anything which is opposed to the qualities that reside in Him. For example, since wisdom and fairness reside in God, He never acts unwisely or unfairly, nor can He. That kind of justice, which, as we have seen above, is called in the Bible, not justice but severity or revenge or by other names of the same type, this I say, as far as it is opposed to mercy, is nothing else than to punish offences.— Besides, it appears that neither the justice nor mercy, of which we are speaking, reside in God whence we read, 'God is slow to anger, and of great mercy,' (Exod. 34:6, Num. 14:18) which manifestly indicates that these two are the effects of His will, the one of which (mercy) greatly surpasses the other, etc." [8]

FREE OBEDIENCE

With the necessity for satisfying an inexorable justice removed, the next step for Socinus was to deny the substitionary atonement of Christ on the Cross. In the *Lectures*, he attacks the conventional doctrine on four main points. It is unethical, he holds, because it excludes the divine mercy; it is impossible, in that it involves the substitution of penalty; it is inadequate, as the sufferings of Christ on the Cross, however great, were finite and insufficient to cover the sin of the whole world; and finally it is absurd, because Christ's obedience was valid for his own exaltation but could not be transferred to others.[9]

To these objections, in the *Concerning the Saver*, Socinus adds the further point that the conventional doctrines of satisfaction and imputation were incompatible. If Christ's death canceled the indictment against man for sin, then it was not necessary for man to appropriate salvation by faith. If the atonement is to be regarded as a transaction, "what's done is done," then further effort upon the part of man is gratuitous. Such an imputed righteousness would do away with the necessity for personal holiness.[10]

Socinus' more constructive position in Christian Soteriology consists in his emphasis upon the need of imitating Christ and attaining the immortality he has vouchsafed to us.

Couet had urged the necessity of imitating

FAUSTUS SOCINUS

Christ, but in his effort to maintain the supreme holiness of Jesus had cautiously qualified the extent to which this was possible. Socinus impatiently brushes aside the cautious disclaimers of his opponent; in speaking of the perfection of God from the text Matthew 5:48, he declares: "It is enough for us to be adorned with a quality of the same kind." And he goes on to say: "That we, therefore, may imitate Christ it is not necessary that we express his most perfect holiness and justice wholly in our life, but that, just as he was holy and just, we should be holy and just, we should even try to equal his innocency most perfectly." Calvin is adduced in support of this position. The paragraph is concluded with the observation that our sins keep cropping out and require constant repression.

This most important section of the *Concerning the Saver* (Part I, Ch. IV) is concluded with the claim that "the way of salvation is to regulate our life according to the example of Christ." In a beautiful passage, Socinus declares: "The supreme pattern of obedience to God, and of love both to God and to men has shone forth in the whole life of Christ." [11]

In the second place (Chapter V), Christ's saving work is made to consist in his showing the way of eternal life by his resurrection, but as this is not so much a way of life as a goal for life, we

FREE OBEDIENCE

have reserved the subject for a more detailed consideration in the following chapter.

Even so orthodox a writer as Shedd, whose succinct account of the Socinian soteriology has been of great assistance to the writer, is forced to concede the clarity of Socinus' objections and to admit the values of Socinus' positive position. "The positive part of Socinus' soteriology is the position that forgiveness is granted upon the ground of repentance and obedience. There are no legal obstacles in the way of pardon, because the will of God is sovereign and supreme over law and penalty. Nothing is necessary, consequently, but sorrow for sin, and an earnest purpose to obey the commandments. Christ has set an example of obedience, and man is to follow in the exercise of his natural powers." [12]

NOTES

1. *Protestant Thought before Kant*, New York, 1911, 107.
2. *Salvation, Eternal Life, Immortality* are synonymous terms for Socinus. See P. 115 ff.
3. The work quoted above was published at Rakow in 1609 and dedicated by Schmalz to the University of Heidelberg. This carefully reasoned treatise covers the whole field of Soteriology and Christian Anthropology and reflects Socinus' mature judgment. The section translated is found in *Opera* I, 553ª.
4. *Opera* I, 541 ff. For a more detailed, but less mature treatment see Socinus' first great controversy, that with Pucci embodied in the disputation: *De Statu primi hominis ante Lapsum.* (1578), *Opera* II, 253 ff.
5. *Opera* I, 540-541.
6. *Opera* II, 652ª.
7. "This divine justice, which has no limit, is not this of which we speak (the legal justice of orthodoxy), but that which alone, as

has been seen above, is denoted in the sacred writers by the famous name of Justice and which can be called another name—Righteousness and Fairness." *Opera* II, 187ª.
    8. *Opera* II, 186-187.
    9. *Opera* I, 570-573.
  10. *Opera* II, 217.
  11. *A History of Christian Doctrine*, William G. T. Shedd, D. D., New York, 1863, Vol. II, 385-386.

CHAPTER XV

IMMORTALITY, THE GOAL OF LIFE

BOTH in his formal works and in his private correspondence, Socinus repeatedly holds before his readers what he considers to be the great message and goal of Christianity—immortality. Professor Pünjer did not exaggerate when he declared that for the Socinians: "The special promise of Christianity, which determines its high value, is eternal life or endless duration."[1] This immortal life is to be achieved by man and is the divine reward for his obedience to the will of God as revealed in the teaching of Jesus. This teaching is ably summarized in the fifth chapter of Part I of the *Concerning the Saver*.

Socinus' succinct summary of his theology commences with two propositions that illustrate the central importance of immortality in his system, and that describe the conditions of its attainment. "The Christian Religion is the heavenly doctrine teaching the true way of attaining eternal life. This way is nothing else but to obey God in regard to those things which he has taught us through our Lord, Jesus Christ."[2]

Thus immortality is the reward for a righteous

FAUSTUS SOCINUS

life and, conversely, the righteous life is the only condition of immortality. "Briefly, if anyone wishes to know, nothing else is required for the obtaining of eternal life except the observance of Christ's precepts."[3] Orthodox writers were accustomed to employ the word "grace" in describing the divine aid to right living. Socinus avoided the word because he considered that superstitious and magical ideas were attached to it. He preferred to speak of the divine assistance, and this divine aid he divided into two parts—external, the promises of the New Covenant, and internal, the work of God's presence in the believer's heart.[4]

From one point of view the Socinian position made the way of life comparatively simple. To keep the goal—a life of endless duration in the bliss of heaven—before one's eyes, and to fulfil day by day the simple teaching of Jesus, must have seemed an easy yoke and a light burden to many earnest souls who were anxiously concerned, if Calvinists, with the supreme question of whether or not they were numbered among the elect; or if Lutherans, with the question of whether their faith in Christ was sufficient for their eternal salvation. From another viewpoint, however, Socinus made the attainment of salvation more difficult by his strict ethical emphasis, and by removing the elements of supernatural grace insisted on by the Protestantism of his age.

IMMORTALITY, THE GOAL OF LIFE

Socinus' appeal, however, was not to the professional theologian or to the mystic, but to the lay mind which could be satisfied by the thought that a good life would secure the *praemium* of immortality.

Just as the orthodox scheme of salvation had been Christocentric, with the cross at the heart of the gospel, so was Socinus' system Christocentric; but for the cross, he substituted the resurrection. Beard thus summarizes the Socinian position: "The central point of Christ's mission is not His death upon the cross, in which He made satisfaction for the sins of the world, but His resurrection, in which He brought life and immortality to light." [5]

In his controversy with the Jesuits of Posen, Socinus stressed the primary importance of Christ as the author and giver of eternal life: "Christ is life, and even eternal life, since he is the author and giver of eternal life. He is the author of eternal life, or, as in the Greek of Acts 3:15, *archēgos*, namely "leader" or "chief," since he himself first of all was raised from the dead to immortal life, and opened up the approach (*aditus*) to the same life for all others by both His words and deeds, and he was after his death the discoverer (*inventor*) and to some degree also the founder of eternal life." [6]

FAUSTUS SOCINUS

Immortality is for Socinus the great New Testament contribution to religion; for him the Old Testament was silent on this point, and modern scholarship has, in the main, substantiated his position. This does not mean, however, that Socinus held that the Old Testament saints had been excluded from eternal felicity; he held that special provision had been made for them.[7]

Within recent years, Professor J. Y. Simpson of New College, Edinburgh, has published a work entitled: *Man and the Attainment of Immortality*,[8] in which he maintains that immortality is a goal to be achieved and is the gift of God for a victorious life. Those who do not "make the grade" are simply consigned to oblivion. Under such a theory immortality becomes conditional and we have to thank Professor Simpson for coining a useful word, "immortability." Socinus' view is similar, he indulges in no fervid descriptions of the bliss enjoyed in the future by the saved, nor does he attempt to terrify men into righteousness through the fear of future torments. Guichard thus neatly summarizes Socinus' position: "The impious will be annihilated, and thus being deprived of the glory for ever, will also suffer for ever"[9]—an explanation that appears more ingenious than straightforward. Socinus in his early work against Pucci had stoutly maintained that St. Paul had meant by "death"

IMMORTALITY, THE GOAL OF LIFE

simply mortality or natural death.[10] In other places he maintained that it was absurd to say that God would eternally punish sins that were not infinite in nature, and that it was an unworthy conception of God to hold that He would eternally continue His wrath against mere creatures.

Socinus' personal attitude toward immortality, in epistles or remarks to friends, is both interesting and helpful. Writing as he states in a letter to Dudicz, "in the middle of life's course," (1583) and surrounded with dangers upon every side, he reminds his friend of "those words which are worthy to be written in golden letters: 'But to me nothing appears to me to be at all lasting, which has some limit; for when that arrives, then what has passed has vanished, that only remains which you have acquired by virtue and by doing right.'"[11]

When on his death-bed twenty years later, worn with strife and labor, Socinus looked forward with confidence and almost eagerness to the death that he felt would bring with it "a release from his trials and the recompense of his labors."[12] The goal was in sight, and the tired athlete felt that he would undoubtedly receive the wreath from the Judge that he had trusted.

NOTES

1. *History of the Christian Philosophy of Religion*, Bernhard Pünjer (translated by Hastie), Edinburgh, 1887, 205.

FAUSTUS SOCINUS

2. The little *Summa Religionis Christianae, Opera* I, 281ª.
3. From a letter to Radecki, *Opera* I, 375ª.
4. See *Racovian Catechism*, V-10 and compare Guichard's excellent summary, op. cit., 390.
5. *The Reformation,* London, 1883, 277. Cf. Socinus' own statement in the *Concerning the Saver* I:5, *Opera* II, 131ª, "The main point, therefore, and as it were, the foundation of all faith, and of our salvation in Christ's person, is the resurrection of Jesus Christ, himself."
6. *Opera* II, 655ᵇ.
7. Chapter V: 6 of the *Quod Regni Poloniae & etc.* deals with this distinction between the two testaments, *Opera* I, 704.
8. London, 3rd Edition, 1924.
9. Opus cit., 390.
10. *Opera* I, 343ᵇ.
11. *Opera* I, 509.
12. *Opera* I, "Life."

CHAPTER XVI

TRUE DOCTRINE THE TEST OF THE TRUE CHURCH

WHILE in the form of church organization that he favored, Socinus closely followed the Calvinistic model, his conception of the nature of the church was widely different. The Socinian Church resembled the Calvinistic, from which it derived its Presbyterian form, in that it was governed by pastors (*ministri*) and elders (*seniores*), and was presided over by a representative governing body. As was so often the case on the continent of Europe, where churches of the reformed model were usually minority bodies, there was not the complete scheme of presbyteries, synods, and a general assembly as in Holland, Scotland, and America. Presbyteries and general assemblies are never mentioned in Socinian writings; a general synod meeting annually at various places sufficed for the three hundred (more or less) congregations of the widely scattered Socinian Church.

A minister is to be chosen by each congregation, it is he "who explains the word of God to others and exhorts them to true piety and holiness of life." The authority of the minister is considerable, but should be used with discretion in accordance with Paul's advice to Timothy and Titus.[1]

The arguments used by Socinus for the validity of the Presbyterian eldership were in perfect accord with the teaching of Calvin. Each elder is to exercise his best gifts in the service of the church, whether it be teaching, discipline, caring for the poor, or church administration. On a minor point, however, there is a difference; the care of the poor is to be entrusted not to a separate body (the diaconate) but to certain of the elders.[2]

The Reformation had brought with it an unending controversy on the true notes of the church. The Catholics uniformly appealed to the authority of the papacy to and the argument from apostolic succession. They affirmed, moreover, that the Nicene notes of unity, sanctity, catholicity, and apostolicity were to be found in the Church of Rome alone. Against this Catholic authoritarianism, Socinus composed a characteristically Protestant tract: *The Catholics can by no means defend their dogmas and rites by the authority of the church.*[3] Socinus avers that the Catholics have departed widely from the teaching and practice of the primitive church, and argues that the church as such is not inerrant; but where the saving doctrine of Christ is taught,

THE TEST OF THE TRUE CHURCH

there is the true church. Scripture, not tradition, is the sole authority for the church, nor does ecclesiastical rank justify the promulgation of a doctrine. In another little tract: *Concerning the Notes of the Church*,[4] Socinus declares that the conventional notes are not to be found in the Catholic Church of his day, and that further, "notes" are not even mentioned by Christ or the apostles. In a short treatise entitled *Concerning Succession*,[5] Socinus anticipates the typical nonconformist arguments against the authority of apostolic succession: "The true church cannot be proved from the succession of persons and places, that is in the same places," he avers, "but only from the succession of doctrine." Commenting upon Christ's command to Peter, "Feed my sheep," always a favorite proof-text of Catholic controversialists, Socinus considers the claim: "that the Roman Pontiff is the universal shepherd (*pastor*) of the whole church of Christ," and maintains that "because anyone is a shepherd, it does not consequently follow that he gives good and healthful food to the sheep." Belief in papal infallibility which had already begun to appear, is denied by Socinus in a rather elaborate argument, in which he attempts to show that a universal bishop would be no more infallible than the bishop of a particular church, because the church as a whole and not any individual is the ultimate authority.[6]

These arguments adduced appear quite in line with Calvinist or Lutheran teaching until we push them, as did Socinus, to their logical conclusions. If Socinus denied both the presence and the validity of the Catholic notes, he also denied the efficacy of the Protestant notes. Calvin and Luther, like Socinus, had emphasized the preaching of the word, but they had added to this the correct observance of the two sacraments, baptism and the Lord's Supper. Socinus with his basic conception of the Church as the organ of true doctrine, denied that either the preaching of the word or the right administration of the sacraments constituted "notes" in the proper sense. The preaching of the word was, for him, the very essence of the Church, and the sacraments were to him simply a corollary of right doctrine.[7]

Socinus, in his view of the sacraments, is the most thoroughly rationalistic of all the reformers, not excluding Zwingli. Several short treatises, largely controversial and concerned principally with baptism, were written by Socinus on the sacraments. The strong Anabaptist strain in the earlier stage of the Polish Antitrinitarian Movement was continually cropping out, and Socinus felt himself obliged to combat what he deemed to be trivial or superstitious practices.[8] His positive

THE TEST OF THE TRUE CHURCH

views are neatly summed up in two sections of the rather lengthy epistle included in the *Concerning the Church* from which we have frequently quoted. The Lord's Supper is a simple memorial, instituted by Christ, in which his followers commemorate his death and render thanks for the same.[9] Baptism is not a perpetual ordinance, but simply a kind of initiation ceremony for converts to the Christian faith. It is not a requisite for entrance into the church.

This position, essentially the same as that of the Quakers, was unusually advanced for Socinus' day and provoked the opposition of many writers who were in other respects in agreement with his views.[10] Socinus was not followed in this extreme view by the later Socinian Church, which recognized the validity and necessity of baptism as the sign of entrance into the Christian fellowship.[11]

At first sight, Socinus' conception of the church appears quite in line with Calvin's teaching. In one of the noblest portions of the *Institutes*,[12] Calvin had declared that the universal church was comprehensive and embraced the righteous of every time and place. The state of the believer and not his official connection with any church constituted his membership in the true church. There is, however, an underlying difference between the two conceptions, for with all its appearance of broadness, the Calvinistic Church is restricted to the elect or those who have been predestined by God to salvation. This restriction is not admitted by Socinus, who in one of his finest passages declares "that nothing else is required for the constituting of the visible (*aspectabilis*) Church of Christ, except the true knowledge of the precepts of Christ, seeing that in Christ, as Paul says (I Cor. 7:19, Gal. 6:15), nothing is of value except a new creature and the observance of the commands of God, which he evidently gives us through Christ, which may be summarized as faith which works through love (*dilectio*) (Gal. 5:6). For in love alone are all the precepts of Christ contained. And John says (I John 2:10) that they who love the brethren remain in the light and there is no stumbling in them, and they are translated from death to life. Briefly, if anyone wishes to know, nothing else is required for the obtaining of eternal life, except the observance of Christ's precepts. Who indeed would dare deny that the true visible Church of Christ is that which holds the doctrine that is sufficient for the pursuit of eternal salvation?"[18]

To use the Anglican phraseology, Socinus' view of the Church is "low," as consisting of a free and open fellowship of those who profess the simple teaching of Jesus. This doctrine from another point of view is truly a high one, as it makes the character of the Church depend entirely upon

THE TEST OF THE TRUE CHURCH

the loyalty of its members to the teaching of Jesus. In many respects Socinus anticipates the present-day tendency to sink sectarian differences in a larger fellowship, the bond of union of which is the common loyalty of all its members to Christ as the Divine Teacher.

NOTES

1. See *Concerning the Choosing and Appointment of Ministers* in the epistle *Concerning the Church* (*Opera* I, 347).

Müller, Op. cit., IV-2-2, 133, rightly observes that the real authority often lay with the local noble who was the patron of the congregation.

2. See an excerpt from another epistle under the general heading *Concerning the Church*, (*De Ecclesia*) *Concerning the Elders of the Church*. (*Opera* I, 351). Socinus' wisdom in providing for a single lay body to act with the pastor in the government and administration of the congregation is approved by the recent tendency in Presbyterian Churches to abandon the diaconate as a separate body.

3. *Opera* I, 323. Note the similarity of Socinus' teaching on this subject to the Augsburg Confession, Art. VII.

4. *Opera* I, 342^a.

5. *Opera* I, 341-342.

6. *Opera* I, 342^a.

7. "The Notes of the Church which the Evangelicals set up, namely, the preaching of the true teaching (*doctrina*) of Christ, and the practice (*usus*) of the Sacraments, are of no value, since they are the very essence of the Church. As regards the first, just this is required, that the true teaching of Christ may be there. The other is consequently superfluous, for where the true teaching is, there is also, of necessity, the true practice of the Sacraments."

Opera I, 342^a.

8. On the Supper, see *Opera* I, 753-775. On Baptism, see *Opera* I, 350-351, 429, and especially 708-752.

9. The 8th Article of the Synod of Lublin (1593) expressed the official position of the Polish (Minor Reformed Unitarian) Church, and shows its close affinity with Socinus' doctrine. "The end and scope of the Lord's Supper is the commemoration and proclamation of the death of Christ. . . . . But as regards the eating of Christ's body, and the drinking of his blood, in no way in the Lord's Supper itself do we eat the body of Christ, and drink his blood, neither corporally, *nor spiritually*, nor otherwise."

It may be added that Socinus made no claim to originality in the doctrine of the Lord's Supper which he held. He repeatedly refers to Zwingli, and of Cellarius or Borrhaüs declares: "But if anyone may

FAUSTUS SOCINUS

have the little book of Martin Cellarius or Borrhaüs, *On the Works of God,* he will have enough, unless my memory fails me, to recognize that my opinion is neither new, nor heard for the first time in our age." *Opera* I, 767^b. See also the *Third Epistle to Niemojewsky, Opera* I, 423.

10. Cf. the controversies with Dudicz (*Opera* I, 738ff) and Czechowitz (*Opera* I, 748ff).

11. The Racovian Catechism composed shortly after the death of Socinus allotted a definite place in its scheme to baptism as the rite of initiation into the church. (V-3).

12. Book IV, Ch. 1, Sec. 7-11.

13. *Opera* I, 374-375 (Letter to Radecki).

CHAPTER XVII

SOCINUS AND RELIGIOUS TOLERANCE

IN AN age marked by a self-conscious and increasing despotism in the affairs of both state and church, Charles the Fifth, Emperor of the Holy Roman Empire, stands, or rather sits, as a type of the political conservatism and religious traditionalism that attempted to stifle the growing freedom and individualism. To Charles, the Empire rested on authority equally divine with that of the Papacy, and on these twin pillars was built the whole fabric of society. Later tradition has pictured the old emperor in a repentant mood in the quiet retirement of the cloister. We are told that Charles amused himself by attempting to synchronize a number of the crude watches of that period, and being constantly thwarted in the attempt finally gave up the task in disgust with the exclamation: "What a fool have I been to neglect my own concerns, and to waste my whole life in a vain attempt to make all men think alike on matters of religion, when I cannot even make a few watches keep time together."

Charles' successors never seem to have learned

the lesson of the incident just mentioned; indeed, the period following the Reformation showed a tightening of religious dogmatism all along the line. This emphasis upon orthodoxy was not confined to the Catholics alone, for if conformity was their watchword, uniformity was the goal of the Protestants. The principle *Cujus regio, ejus religio* while applied most strictly in the Holy Roman Empire was widely used as a working basis outside, and minorities fared badly. Both Catholics and Protestants, not satisfied with persuasion or even discipline within the church, were quick to resort to the secular arm in the states where they were officially recognized, and cases of bitter persecution and even execution on the part of Lutherans directed against the Reformed are on record,[1] while both groups united to suppress with the utmost severity the radicals, whether social, as the Anabaptists, or religious, as the Socinians. Even the best offices of Calvin and Melanchthon to achieve something like unity between the two great Protestant communions were on the whole unsuccessful.

Still later in the seventeenth century we find the spirit of tolerance fiercely assailed by Catholic and Protestant alike with only a brave spirit here and there to speak a word for toleration. In England, Jeremy Taylor and Chillingworth among the Episcopalians and Baxter among the

RELIGIOUS TOLERANCE

Presbyterians were like voices crying in the wilderness amid the clamor of civil and religious strife. Even on his deathbed the saintly Chillingworth was tormented by the narrow Puritan divine, Cheynell,[2] who railed against him for not denouncing the Socinians with his last breath.[3] Baxter drew upon himself the wrath of his stricter colleagues while attending a council at London during the Protectorate. He had composed a "declaration of fundamentals" remarkable for its deep piety and its generous spirit, but it was vehemently opposed on the grounds that any Socinian or papist could subscribe to such a statement; to which Baxter nobly replied, "So much the better, and so much the better is it to be the matter of concord."[4]

The great majority of both Catholic and Protestant churchmen were unalterably opposed to tolerance either in principle or in practice. The admirable and eloquent Bossuet declared in a classic Catholic apologetic: "There is no more dangerous illusion than to give tolerance as a mark of the true church, and among Christians, the Socinians, and the Anabaptists are the only ones who oppose this doctrine."[5] On the other hand, Bossuet's opponent, the author of *Rights of the Two Sovereigns*, etc., terms universal toleration "this Socinian dogma—the most dangerous of all those of the Socinian sect, since it is going to ruin Christianity and establish impartiality (*indifference*) between religions." [6]

Beza, who conducted a long-drawn-out controversy with the Italian exiles, Chateillon (Castalio) and Aconzio,[7] held that the civil magistrate was bound to inflict the death penalty on those who maintained heretical doctrines on the Trinity, and his view was in general common alike to Catholics and Protestants, and if Italy, Spain, France and Poland executed such offenders, Protestant states such as England, Scotland, and even Geneva and Bern had their quota of Unitarian martyrs.

All of this general survey proclaims the fact that the Socinians, so often the victims of relentless persecution, were as a group among the very first, if not in fact, the very first, to proclaim the need for universal toleration in matters of religion. Isolated figures in the earlier stages of the Reformation, Aconzio and others among the Italians, and Hübmaier [8] and certain other Anabaptists, had previously agitated the cause of religious tolerance, but the Socinians appear to have been the first religious body to have advocated this principle.

Socinus, himself, seems to have been directly responsible for this breadth of outlook among his followers. It is easy, of course, to say that a minority leader in religion is always tolerant in or-

RELIGIOUS TOLERANCE

der to secure the perpetuation of his own sect and ideas, but as a matter of history this has not always been the case, for the spirit of numerous religious minorities and their leaders has been bigoted to the extreme. Socinus' generous attitude seems to be the product of both his humanistic environment and his faithful attempt to reproduce the spirit of Jesus' teaching.

In his last important published work, an address to the "Evangelicals" of Poland and Lithuania, Socinus condemned the bigotry of both Catholics and "Evangelicals" in their attitude toward those who held differing doctrines respecting the Trinity. "But we," he said, "follow a much milder opinion in this respect, and firmly believe that whoever shall have trusted in God and Christ, and shall show himself obedient, will certainly obtain eternal life." [9]

Socinus appears at his best in his correspondence with his friend, Matthew Radecki, superintendent of the Transylvanian churches; in an epistle dated September 24, 1584, he gives his own reasons for adhering to the Antitrinitarian body, and then nobly declares: "I do not condemn other churches, nor by any means despise them, but acknowledge all as the true churches of Christ, in which the voice of the precepts of Jesus Christ our Lord resounds and is heard, even if in certain doctrines which do not relate to the actual precepts,

FAUSTUS SOCINUS

they do not seem to me to think rightly, and whosoever keep the same precepts, I consider to be true members of Christ." [10]

No wonder many of the leaders of the Enlightenment, over a century later, looked back to Socinus as the harbinger of a new era, and it is surprising that only a few of our modern historians, such as Lecky, have given adequate recognition to the pioneer work done by Socinus in the field of religious liberty.

NOTES

1. The persecution of Laski's refugee congregation which had fled from London may be instanced. This action did much to dampen Calvin's eager efforts to achieve an agreement with the Lutherans. Still more extreme is the case of Nicholas Krell who was convicted of disseminating Calvinistic doctrine in Lutheran Saxony and was executed at Dresden in 1601. See Engelcken, *Dissertatio de Nic. Crellio, Ejusque Supplicio*, Rostock, 1724.

2. The author of the *Rise, Growth, and Danger of Socinianism* (1643).

3. See Gardner's *The Puritan Revolution*, London, 1883, p. 134-135.

4. See *Encyclopaedia Britannica*, 11th Ed., III, 552ᵃ. It is only right to add, however, that Baxter's aim was not so much a group of mutually tolerant sects as a comprehensive church that would be inclusive enough to embrace all sects.

5. *Protestant Variations*, Book 10, Ch. 56.

6. From the *Droits des deux Souverains* etc., published at Rotterdam, 1687, p. 14. The author appears to have been the well-known Reformed apologist, Jurieu, pastor of the French congregation at Rotterdam.

7. The well-known engineer who labored in London for many years and dedicated his celebrated work, *Collection of the Stratagems of Satan* (Basel, 1565) to Queen Elizabeth. This book in defence of religious tolerance was fiercely assailed by the Calvinists and held in high regard by Arminius. It went through numerous editions and translations.

8. See *Balthasar Hübmaier*, Henry C. Vedder, New York, 1905. His important tract on tolerance, *On Heretics and their Burning* is reprinted entire in this work, p. 84 (1524).

RELIGIOUS TOLERANCE

9. *Quod Regni Poloniae & Magni Ducatus Lithuaniae Homines,* etc. *Opera* I, p. 700^b.

10. *Opera* I, 373^a. The similarity of Grotius' conclusion to his *De Veritate* is striking: "And as to those who in some things think otherwise than we do, we are to wait till God shall make the hidden truth manifest unto them; in the meantime, we are to hold fast, and fulfil those things we are agreed in. Now we know in part; the time will come, when all things shall be most certainly known." (Bk. VI, Sec. II, Clarke's translation).

CHAPTER XVIII

SOCINUS AND PACIFISM

EVERY student of primitive Christianity is acquainted with the pacifist position of the early church. Recruits such as the young African, Maximilianus, and veterans such as the centurion, Marcellus, who refused to bear arms because of their Christian principles, were executed, and one of the commonest objections to the growing sect was that its adherents were unwilling to employ force in preserving the strength of the state, whether in civic or military capacities.

With the official recognition of Christianity a great change came in the attitude of the church toward war. As Devere Allen remarks: "From the time when Constantine made Christianity his imperial handmaid in 312 A.D. only a 'remnant' in every generation carried on the original nonviolent way of life."[1]

The Reformation did not bring peace but a sword, and its leaders were constrained either by temperament or by necessity to advocate the use of force to protect and propagate the new churches. Luther's attitude toward Rome can

SOCINUS AND PACIFISM

scarcely be termed pacific, but nowhere does his irascible spirit appear in a worse light than in his manifesto directed at the peasants of South Germany when they revolted against their tyrannical overlords.[2] Zwingli felt compelled to take up the sword in the defence of the Reformed Church in Switzerland and actually perished upon the battlefield of Kappel. Even Calvin, whose zeal for peace exceeded that of most men of his day, would not go so far as to condemn armed self-defence, and warmly supported the Huguenots in the religious war of 1562.[3]

Although the major sects of the Reformation were no more pacifist than was the Church of Rome, a number of smaller groups, despite continual persecution, proclaimed an uncompromising pacifism. The original Anabaptists and later sects like the Schwenkfelders, Dunkards, and Quakers labored with the Socinians to revive the early Christian ideal. In Poland the efforts of Menno among the Anabaptists coupled with the pacifist opinions of most of the early Antitrinitarians had prepared the way for Socinus, whose doctrine here and elsewhere gave shape to ideas already current but not formally enunciated.

The pacifism of Socinus was grounded upon a thoroughgoing rejection of violence in all forms, and is rather one of the most significant elements of a general non-violent program than an isolated ideal. Hence we often find in the writings of Socinus, first a general condemnation of anger or strife and then a denuciation of war, capital punishment, murder, private feuds, etc.

In his early commentary on the Sermon on the Mount, Socinus lays down his general position in his treatment of the beatitude, "Blessed are the peacemakers." After a scholarly investigation as to the meaning of "peacemakers," in which the Latin, Greek, and Hebrew forms of the word are carefully weighed, Socinus observes: "For of these he (Christ) says that they shall be called sons of God, which certainly seems to accord with zeal for peace and its observance, inasmuch as it is fitting for God to be called the God of peace in Paul who fittingly opposes peace, the author of which is God, to discord and dissension in the First Epistle to the Corinthians, Ch. 14." [4]

Guichard, whose impartiality we have previously noted, in his summary of Socinus' leading ideas under the heading of *Sur la Morale*, neatly summarises the non-violent elements of Socinus' teaching in a group of pithy propositions:

"That it is not permitted a Christian to make war nor even to go to war under the authority and command of a prince, nor even to employ the assistance of a magistrate in order to secure vengeance for an affront which he has received."

SOCINUS AND PACIFISM

"That to make war is always to do evil, and to act contrary to the precept of Jesus Christ."

"That a Christian can not exercise the office of magistrate, if in this capacity he must use violence."

And finally the extreme positions:

"That it is not permitted Christians to defend their life, nor that of others by force, even against robbers and other enemies, if they can defend it otherwise; because it is impossible that God would permit a truly pious man, and one who trusted in Him with sincerity, to find himself in these disturbing situations where he should wish to save himself at the expense of his neighbor's life."

"That the murder of one's aggressor is a greater crime than the murder committed in taking vengeance; in avenging oneself, one only makes it even; but in the other case, namely in preventing a thief or an enemy, one kills a man who had only the desire to frighten, in order to steal more easily."[5]

Socinus rejoiced in the agreement of others with him in his extreme pacifist position. In a letter to Schmalz, under date of Dec. 2, 1599, he congratulates his friend on his adherence to the Pauline principle that "a Christian man is not allowed to war against men."[6] "Our warfare is spiritual and not carnal," continues Socinus, "and is against Satan and not man."

It was the controversy with Palaeologus, however, that brought forth Socinus' classic on non-violence, the *De Magistratu* to which we have already alluded and from which Guichard drew the five *sententiae* noted above.

Palaeologus had argued that "The precepts of Christ about loving our enemies did not have the force of never permitting us to kill our enemies." He had further claimed that it was a laudable action for God to slay the wicked and that "when a bad man was killed by the authority of the magistrate, or in battle, or for some other reason, it was by the command of God."

Socinus replied with fine sarcasm that the precepts of Christ on love were spoken not for the benefit of God, but man, and that if Palaeologus was speaking to the point he would have to prove that the very enemies who were slain by us, were to be loved. On no grounds can capital punishment or war be justified is Socinus' uncompromising position.[7]

In Parts III and IV of this lengthy defence, Socinus strongly resists the attempts made by his opponent to defend war in certain cases. Palaeologus' arguments from proof texts of Scripture are very adequately refuted *seriatim*, and Socinus falls back again and again upon his basic

SOCINUS AND PACIFISM

position that the love which Christ commands us to have for our enemies prohibits us under any circumstances from taking human life.

Later scholars looking back upon the brief glory and ultimate collapse of the Socinian Church in Poland were wont to attribute its failure to legal and military objections. Bayle, who often betrays a covert sympathy with the Socinians, observes: "Whence one ought to conclude that the Socinian religion is not made for a whole people, nor for the majority; it is suited only to certain choice temperaments; and if it is true that one of the popes upon hearing it said that the Protestants would not allow adultery or fornication, exclaimed that they would not last for long, one may be assured that his prediction would have been more to the point, had it been applied to a sect which renounces arms and dignities." [8]

Was Bayle right? If so, let us not scorn a church that was so true to the Sermon on the Mount that it suffered itself to be sacrificed upon the altar of nationalism rather than betray its trust. The blood of the martyrs is truly the seed of the church, and the self-abnegation of the Socinians, Mennonites, Quakers and other persecuted religious minorities, seems at last to be bearing fruit in helping to bring about a warless world.

FAUSTUS SOCINUS

NOTES

1. Article *Pacifism, Old and New* in *Pacifism in the Modern World,* New York, 1930, VIII.
2. "After speaking about the duties of the authorities, he proceeds: 'In the case of an insurgent, every man is both judge and executioner. Therefore, whoever can should knock down, strangle, and stab such publicly or privately, and think nothing so venomous, pernicious, and devilish as an insurgent. . . . Such wonderful times are these, that a prince can merit heaven better with bloodshed than another with prayer.'" T. M. Lindsay, *History of the Reformation,* Edinburgh (Second Edition), Vol. I, p. 337, footnote I.
3. In all justice it must be said that Calvin's spirit was admirable in this strife which was marked by so much bloodshed and ill-will. Henry (op. cit., II, 409) says: "Calvin's oft-repeated sentiments show clearly how earnestly he endeavoured to calm the excited feelings of his associates. Thus he declared to them, that "if they wished to establish their rights by the sword, they would prevent God from helping them."—"One single drop of blood shed by you will overflow all France." He forbade their taking possession of the churches; and said, "that he should be not less indignant than the king against those who employed violence." In two of his letters to Soubize, the leader in the movement, he directed him to lay down his arms, as the king desired, and to submit himself to the legitimate authority of the state. He regarded it as something especially monstrous for ministers of religion to bear arms: "It is their duty to believe that the church will be extended by other and extraordinary means." He included the duke of Guise in the number of those for whom he prayed. . . . Thus notwithstanding the accusation of hostile polemics, there still remains inscribed on the standard which he raised, the apostolic motto: "The weapons of our warfare are not carnal, but spiritual."
4. *Opera* I, 3^b. Socinus' analysis of "pacem facientes" as active efforts directed toward the achievement of peace has a very modern ring.
5. Op. cit., 391-392.
6. *Opera* I, 463^a.
7. For the discussion just quoted see II, 33-34.
8. Op. cit., Note, 171. It cannot be doubted that the pacifistic attitude of the Socinians, during the Cossack War of 1648 and the Swedish War of 1657, did much to incite the active measures that led to their expulsion from Poland.

CHAPTER XIX

THE CONTINUING INFLUENCE OF SOCINUS

THE Golden Age of Socinianism in Poland may be dated from 1588 to 1627; this period commences with the important Synod of Brest-Litowsk, at which the warring factions of the Unitarians became united under the leadership of Socinus, and closes with the first serious blow struck at the Socinian Church after its rise to power, the expulsion of the Socinians from Lublin and the destruction of their property there.

The death of Socinus in 1604 in no wise hindered the growth of the church for which he had exhausted himself in ceaseless activity. The Racovian catechism on which he had labored was brought to completion and published in 1605. The school at Rakow grew in influence and importance, its faculty, comprising such scholars as Christopher Ostorod, Valentine Schmalz, the Lubieniecki brothers, John Krell, Peter Morzkowski, and Martin Ruarus, was known all over central and eastern Europe and its liberal, practical curriculum attracted students from many lands and faiths. Continued efforts were made to effect a *rapprochement* with the Calvinists and Lutherans, but the more orthodox sects were sympathetic only when suffering persecution along with the Socinians. When the full weight of official and Jesuit pressure was brought to bear upon the radicals, they cravenly disavowed all fellowship with them.

During all this period Socinianism was spread far and wide throughout the country; whereas the original seat of the Church had always been in Little Poland, a gradual shift eastward was noticeable, owing perhaps as much to persecution as to propaganda. In Volhynia, under the patronage of the powerful Hoyski family, and ably headed first by Stanislaus Wiszowaty (the husband of Agnes Sozzini) and later by his son, Andrew, the Socinians established many churches, notably at Robkow, Kurczyck, and Hosczca. Even the distant province of Kieff on the Russian border included Socinian churches. White Russia also counted scattered Socinian groups where local magnates and some noble ladies welcomed the emissaries of the new movement and established churches. Far to the south on the Hungarian frontier, Luslawice, the scene of Socinus' last days and his final resting place, became the mother of several smaller communities. In Great Poland and Livonia the movement was, for

CONTINUED INFLUENCE

the most part, captured by the Lutherans, while in Central Poland (e. g. Wegrow) and in Lithuania proper, the Reformed Church got the upper hand.[1] The strength of the Socinian church in its heyday may be gathered from the following figures supplied by Wilbur.[2] The Synod of Rakow of 1612 was attended by 400 delegates; six years later 459 attended another synod at the same place. The names of 115 churches are still on record, and the total number of congregations may be estimated at not less than 300.

The growing power of the church, and its endless debates with the Jesuits, who were often worsted, to say nothing of its complete lack of sympathy with the growing spirit of nationalism, brought down a long series of official actions against the Socinians. Not merely their heretical opinions, but what was much more serious in the eyes of the government, their lack of civic spirit and their failure to engage actively in the Swedish wars formed the chief charges brought against them. A thoughtless prank on the part of some students was the pretext for closing the school at Rakow and for the confiscation of its printing plant (1638). Finally, in the year 1658, the Diet of Warsaw published an edict declaring that it was a capital offence to profess Socinian doctrines or to harbor Socinians, the latter clause being directed primarily against the numerous noble patrons of the sect. Three years, subsequently reduced to two, were allowed members of the sect to settle their affairs and leave the country.[3] Great efforts were made by some of the leaders, notably Stanislaus Lubieniecki, to procure an asylum for the exiles in some foreign land, but with little success. Transylvania received a large colony of the refugees, but as the way led through hostile territory many of the exiles perished from exposure or abuse *en route*. Polish Socinian congregations, however, continued to exist for several generations in this friendly environment until finally merged in the local Unitarian body. The Duke of Brieg in Silesia hospitably received a considerable body of refugees in his town of Kreutzburg, and this place became a ***rendezvous*** for refugees. Brandenburg, Prussia, Holland, and England also received scattered groups of the refugees and generally tolerated them, provided they existed *sub rosa*. Despite a degree of official persecution the Socinians in Holland managed to have their classic corpus of writings, the ***Bibliotheca Fratrum Polonorum*** published under date of 1656.[4]

While the last distinctly Socinian congregation was disbanded in Prussia at the close of the eighteenth century, and the last persons officially registered as Socinians died in the middle of the following century, it cannot be said that Socin-

CONTINUED INFLUENCE

ianism had slowly died out without deeply influencing the religious thought of Protestantism. Unitarian historians, such as Allen, Wilbur, and Gow, trace the connection between modern Unitarians and the seventeenth century Socinians, but more significant still is the steady stream of hostile literature that poured forth from the presses of orthodox theologians from the days of Socinus down into the nineteenth century. Zealous defenders of orthodoxy, whether Protestant or Catholic, have been quick to notice the presence and prevalence of Socinian opinions in the ranks of the faithful, and this has been the chief cause for their concern.

"Crypto-Socinianism" had a great vogue in the latter half of the seventeenth and the first half of the eighteenth centuries.[5] Bayle quotes the anonymous author of *La Politique du Clergé de France*, whose main point is that the chief danger to French Catholicism did not consist in the Protestant opposition, but in the Socinians in the church. This author goes on to say: "And what is more terrible is that this is not merely the religion of our young abbés, it is the theology of certain weighty and learned societies and those who make a great parade of the purity of their life and of their attachment for the Catholic faith." The writer evidently had the Port-Royalists in mind, and the famous Antoine Arnauld hastened to publish a denial of the prevalence of such views. That this Socinian strain persisted in the French church is, however, indubitable, and the *Éclaircissement* of the eighteenth century, while laying a new emphasis upon nature, republished many of the distinctive tenets of Socinianism.

In Germany, Socinianism had gained a considerable foothold even before the collapse of the movement in Poland. The University of Altdorf, owing to the efforts of one of the professors, a certain Ernest Sohner, became a hotbed of the doctrines; some of the students won over by Sohner later became leaders in the Socinian Church. Among their number were John Krell, Martin Ruarus, and Samuel Przypkowski, and the movement spread to Nuremberg; the prompt action of the magistrates, however, stifled the growing sect, and its adherents were either silenced or expelled (1616).[6] The Socinian exiles, however, do not seem to have exerted any considerable influence in Prussia or Brandenburg, where they had settled, and the two Sands, father and son, who were undoubtedly influenced by the movement, were not Socinians so much as Arians.

It is difficult to say how much nineteenth century German theology owes to Socinus and his school. Despite their searching criticisms of Socinianism it is impossible not to discover many of

CONTINUED INFLUENCE

the Socinian viewpoints re-appearing in such writers as Ritschl and Harnack. That these emphases were the product of a new age rather than a conscious harking back to Socinus is indubitable, but it is interesting to trace the parallels.

In Great Britain the Socinian strain appears more strongly marked. John Biddle (1615-1662), termed by Toulmin the "father of the English Unitarians," while departing from the teaching of Socinus on several points, evinced a great admiration for the latter. Biddle translated the Racovian Catechism and Przypkowski's biography which he had published (1653).

Lardner and many of the right-wing deists of the subsequent century held views that accorded generally with those of Socinus, and despite strenuous opposition from the orthodox, the movement grew apace. The famous Joseph Priestley, despite the opprobrium attached to the name[7], made no objection to the designation of Socinian, and reproduced essentially the system of Socinus.[8]

A brief work of this nature cannot pretend to go into all the ramifications of the later trends of Socinianism in Unitarianism, Universalism, and liberal Protestant thought generally. Suffice it to say that many positions often considered novel and epoch-making, such as Macleod Campbell's

FAUSTUS SOCINUS

theory of the Atonement,[9] Ritschl's avoidance of the dogma of the Trinity, and the modern emphasis on the Christian ethic, to say nothing of the current trend toward absolute pacifism, are anticipated by three hundred years in the writings of a theologian who has been consistently maligned, misunderstood, or ignored.

The object of the present writer has been to rescue from comparative obscurity a thinker whom he considers to be one of the most fearless and original and at the same time, one of the sanest and, indirectly, one of the most influential figures of the Reformation and its sequel. Should this slender work tempt any reader to make a more thorough investigation of the life or literary remains of Faustus Socinus, the author would feel amply repaid for any labor he has expended.

NOTES

1. The foregoing summary of the extent of the Socinian Church in Poland is taken largely from Lubieniecki's *History,* Chs. 12-16.

2. Op. cit., 153. Cf. Wallace, op. cit., I, lix.

3. A vivid picture of the sufferings and, in some instances, the martyrdom of the Polish Socinians can be gained from Lubieniecki, Chs. 17-18, and the appendices to Sand's *Bibliotheca,* especially the *Epistola de Wissowatii Vita* and Przypkowski's *Equitis Poloni Vindiciae,* etc.

4. This was accomplished through the efforts of Andrew Wiszowaty and is a monument to the skill and art of seventeenth century typography. The printer was the well-known Dutch champion of rational religion, Franz Kuyper. Besides the works of Socinus which comprise the first two volumes in the series, three later Socinian writers are represented, John Krell, Schlichting, and Wolzogen.

5. Bayle, opus cit., 170, declares: "His sect, very far from dying with him, multiplied thereafter considerably: but since it was ex-

pelled from Poland in the year 1658, it has greatly fallen away—it is greatly diminished as regards its visible state; but on the other hand there are not a few people who are persuaded that it has increased invisibly, and that it is becoming more numerous every day."

6. See G. G. Zeltner, *Historia Crypto-Socinismi Altorfinae Quondam Academiae infesti Arcana,* Leipzig, 1729, 2 vols.

7. Numerous tracts, many with amusing titles, testify to this abhorrence of Socinianism. Andrew Marvel once complained: "No man can tell you the truth, but he must presently be a Socinian." *The Rehearsal Transposed: the Second Part,* London, 1673, 307.

8. Gordon, *The Sozzini and their School, Theol. Rev.* XVI, 531-532, cites the following excerpt from Priestley's *Memoirs* that shows his close connection with Socinus' thought: "By reading with care *Dr. Lardner's Letter on the Logos,* I became what is called a Socinian soon after my settlement at Leeds (1767, aet. 34); and after giving the closest attention to the subject, I have seen more and more reason to be satisfied with that opinion to this day, and likewise to be more impressed with the idea of its importance."

9. *The Nature of the Atonement,* London, 1895, esp. 150ff. Cf. Bushnell's *Vicarious Sacrifice,* New York, 1891.

BIBLIOGRAPHY

SOCINUS, FAUSTUS—*Opera,* in *Bibliotheca Fratrum Polonorum,* Vols. I & II, Amsterdam (1656). Contains everything of importance by the subject of this work. (All the works are in Latin and there is a fairly good index.)

PRZYPKOWSKI, SAMUEL—*Vita Authoris,* prefixed to the above. (Laudatory but substantially accurate.)

SAND, CHRISTOPHER CHRISTOPHORI—*Bibliotheca Antitrinitariorum,* Freistadt, 1684. (A carefully annotated bibliography with valuable appendices on various phases of the movement.)

LUBIENIECKI, STANISLAUS—*Historia Reformationis Polonicae,* Freistadt, 1685. (A gossipy but valuable history of the movement, especially in its later phases—little concerning Socinus.)

GUICHARD, ANASTASE [1]—*Histoire du Socinianisme,* Paris, 1723. (A fair and critical consideration from the Roman Catholic viewpoint.)

BAYLE, PIERRE—*Dictionnaire,* esp. Vol. V, Amsterdam, 1734. (Contains valuable material from earlier sources otherwise inaccessible, not wholly accurate.)

MOSHEIM, J. L.—*Ecclesiastical History, Century XVI,* Ch. 4. Author's last edition, 1755. Reid's edition of 1848 best. (Not entirely fair, but much more adequate in treatment than many later histories.)

BOCK, FRIEDRICH S.—*Historia Antitrinitariorum, Maxime Socinianismi et Socinianorum,* 2 vols., Leipzig, 1774. (A learned compendium of the lives and works of the

BIBLIOGRAPHY

Unitarians from Ochino down to the middle of the eighteenth century; does not include the Socini.)

TOULMIN, JOSHUA—*Memoirs of the Life, Character, Sentiments and Writings of Faustus Socinus,* London, 1777. (Valuable as the only work on Socinus in English, but a eulogy rather than a critical estimate.)

REES, THOMAS—*The Racovian Catechism,* London, 1818. (An excellent translation with an informative introduction.)

TRECHSEL, F.—*Die Protestantischer Antitrinitarier Vor Faustus Socinus,* Heidelberg, 1844. (Valuable notices on the earlier figures, especially Ochino and Laelius Socinus. Contains a valuable appendix of source material, including all the extant opuscula of Laelius.)

FOCK, OTTO—*Der Socinianismus,* Kiel, 1847. (The standard German work on the subject, scholarly and sympathetic, but does not distinguish clearly between Socinus' own teaching and the later Socinians. The approach is synthetic rather than analytical.)

WALLACE, ROBERT—*Antitrinitarian Biography,* 3 vols., London, 1850. (Valuable as an English compendium, but based upon the earlier works of Sand, Bayle, and Bock.)

CANTU, C.—*Gli Eretici d'Italia,* Vol. II, 1866. (The standard work in Italian, containing valuable source material.)

GORDON, ALEXANDER—(1) *The Sozzini and their School,* Theological Review, Vol. XVI, 1879. (Two interesting articles on Laelius and Faustus Socinus, respectively. Shows close acquaintance with Siena.) (2) *Socinus,* Encylopaedia Britannica, IX-XIV Editions. (Articles on Laelius and Faustus; brief but comprehensive.)

BIBLIOGRAPHY

LECLER, F.—*F. Socin,* Geneva, 1884. (Inaccessible work by an unknown author.)

ALLEN, J. H.—*The Unitarians,* New York, 1894. (Interesting chapters on the early phases of the movement.)

HARNACK, ADOLF—*History of Dogma* (English translation), Vol. VII, Boston, 1900. (Valuable estimate, but based almost exclusively on the Racovian Catechism.)

WOTSCHKE, THEODOR—*Geschichte der Reformation in Polen,* Leipzig, 1911. (A succinct history of the Polish Reformation up to 1570.)

MÜLLER, KARL—*Kirchengeschichte,* IV, II, 2., Tübingen, 1919. (Brief but comprehensive and impartial notices on Socinianism and the Reformation in Poland and Lithuania.)

VAN SLEE, J. C.—*De Geschiedvis Van Het Socinianisme in de Nederlanden,* Haarlem, 1914. (The standard work on Socinianism in Holland with a competent summary of Socinian doctrine in the first chapter. Is the only modern work containing the portrait of Socinus.)

WILBUR, EARL MORSE—*Our Unitarian Heritage,* Boston, 1925. (Excellent chapters on the early Unitarians of Poland and Transylvania.)

NOTES

1. This anonymous work is assigned to the well-known Père Lamy, who flourished in the first quarter of the eighteenth century, by the later editors of Mosheim, especially Murdock, whose slighting reference is unmerited. More recent investigations are united in assigning the work to Père Louis-Anastase Guichard. See

Nouvelle Biographie Générale (Michaud), Paris, 1858, XXII, 523.

Dictionnaire des Ouvrages Anonymes, Barbier, Paris, 1874, 2nd Ed., II, 793.

Nomenclator Literarius, Hurter, Innsbruck, 1910, 3rd Ed., IV, Col. 1254.